HANDBOOK FOR CORPORATE LAWYERS.

Esther Chidera, Agbom. LL. B, B.L
Barrister-at-Law

Handbook for Corporate lawyers

Printed and published in Abuja-Nigeria by MultiTech Prints Ltd.

Email: multitechint@gmail.com

Phone: +2349071159887

ISBN: 978-978-783-199-1

PREFACE

Handbook for Corporate Lawyers is an essential guide to every corporate lawyer, providing a friendly yet deep understanding of corporate law practice, particularly incorporation activities. This book aims to create a valuable resource for young corporate practitioners, starting with the history of corporate transactions, creating an accredited agent account, and Incorporation: Pre- and post-incorporation.

Due to the step-by-step clarification and presentation, it is hoped that young lawyers will find it helpful in understanding and carrying out corporate practice.

Overall, my aim with this book is to provide a comprehensive and practical guide to Company's Incorporation. I hope that it unfolds the purposes sought by every reader.

ACKNOWLEDGEMENT

I would like to express my sincere gratitude to God Almighty for the wisdom and strength to write this book "Handbook for Corporate Lawyers: A Practical Guide to Incorporation Activities" This book provides a wealth of practice procedures for anyone enthusiastic about corporate law practice relating to the creation of an accredited agent account, business name, company, and incorporated trustee registration. It also extends to post-incorporation filing of annual returns.

I commend my superiors and colleagues in the practice, academic, and business world for their ideas and research support.

I am very thankful to Dr. Ben Jones Akpan, Barr. Ifeoma Ilodibia, Dr. Sam Peters, Sct. Charles Ugwu, Master Gabriel Chisimdi, and the publisher for their support in bringing this valuable resource to readers.

And finally, to my beloved mother, siblings, and amazing friends who supported me while I toiled in writing this book.

DEDICATION

In the cherished memory of my late father, Mr. Agbom O. Peter.
(For his principles and love for Knowledge.)

TABLE OF CONTENTS

CHAPTER 1

CORPORATE TRANSACTION

1.1   THE HISTORY OF CORPORATE TRANSACTIONS.

A Corporate Transaction involves the transfer of services from one person (a legal or juristic person)[1] to another. See **Bulet INTL (NIG) LTD & Anor v. Olaniyi & Anor,**[2] **Salomon vs Salomon**[3] **United Cement Co. LTD v. Libend Group LTD &Anor.**[4] More like trade, it is the transfer of goods and services (assets) from one person to another.

Trade as a great concept of corporate transactions begun so long before recorded. It could be traced back to the 16th century in Germany, from the barter system where the exchange was not that of monetary end services but an exchange of goods to goods and services to services.

Before the 17th century, goods and services were traded by the British, The Asiento, which allowed for the trading of African slaves to the Spanish and Portuguese Empires. In the 20th Century, the exchange grew beyond the system of trade by barter to retail trade, wholesale, commercial trade, or merchandise that could be on or offline to capture what was best for a competitive transaction.

1.2   THE MODERN CORPORATE PRACTICE

The concept of corporate practice has existed for centuries. The notion did not come into writing until the 16th and 17th centuries. Beginning with the East India Company, the Hudson's Bay Company, the Lavant Company, and other major chattered

---

[1] Incorporated Trustees of Holy Apostles Church, Ayetoro & ORS V. INCD Trustees Oneness Faith of Christ Ministry Ayetoro & ORS (2016) LPELR-41368(CA).
[2] (2017) LPELR-42475 (SC)
[3] (1897) AC. 22
[4] (2016) LPELR-42038 (CA)

companies.[5]

Practically, corporate transactions have been seen as fraudulent and speculative schemes of fraud to the naive and generally to the public. The case of the 17th Century South Sea Company, a British Joint-stock Company founded in January 1711 by John Blunt and John Aislabie and was registered as a public private partnership to consolidate and reduce the cost of the national debt. Which turned out to later be the "world's first financial crash" the world's first Ponzi scheme, speculation mania, and an example of what can happen when people fall prey to groupthink. Even Isaac Newton himself lost as much as £40 million of today's money in the scheme. Up until 1720, the Bubble Act was passed by parliament forbidding the creation of joint-stock companies such as the South Sea Company without the specific performance of a royal charter.[6]

Modern company law came when the two pieces of legislation were codified under the Joint Stock Companies Act 1856 at the behest of the then vice president of the Board of Trade, MR. Robert Lowe.

In 1825 at the repeal of the Bubble Act; it was enacted that in any charter hereinafter to be granted by his majesty, his heirs, and his successors, for the incorporation of any company or body of person, it shall and may be lawful, in and by such charter to be declared and provide, that the members of such corporation shall be individually liable, in their persons and property for the debts, contracts, and engagements of such corporation, to such extent, and subject to such regulation and restriction as his majesty, his heirs and successors, may claim fit and proper, and as shall be declared and limited in and by such charter and the member of such corporation shall whereby be rendered so liable accordingly.[7]

---

[5] Nicholas J.P: https://www.diligent.com/insights/corporate -governance/
[6] The south sea Bubble. https://www.historic-uk.com/HistoryUK/History of England/South-sea-Bubble/
[7] Statutes of the United Kingdom. 1825.

1.3. THE EVOLUTION AND GROWTH OF COMPANY LAW IN NIGERIA.

1.3.1. THE FIRST ORDINANCE.

Companies Ordinance 1912: This was the first local statute to provide for the incorporation of companies by registration. The 1912 Ordinance was based on the UK Companies Act 1908, which was then the current statute of England. Also came the Ordinance to the Colony of Lagos in 1917 which was amended and extended to apply to the whole country.

The 1922 Companies Ordinance amended and consolidated the two ordinances (1912 and the Companies Ordinance of 1917). Sequel to growth in years, the Companies Ordinance of 1922 was subsequently amended and modified successively in (1929, 1941, and 1954).

After the independence in 1960, Nigerians were given freedom by their colonial masters. The first Company Act became the Company Act of 1963, which was a designation of the 1954 Ordinance and was repealed by the 1968 Company Act.

1.3.2   The Companies Act 1968

Noting that the previous Act and Ordinance culled the incessant of unregistered bodies, the Companies Act of 1968 thereby prohibited foreign companies that were not registered in Nigeria from carrying on business in the country. Section 370[8] provides thus.

> **(1)**   Every foreign company within paragraph (b) of Section 368 of this Decree shall give notice in writing of its intention to the register, and as soon

---

[8] Companies Act. Law of the Federation of Nigeria 1968, section 370.

thereafter as may be, the foreign company shall take all steps necessary to obtain incorporation as a separate entity in Nigeria for the purpose aforesaid, but until so incorporated, the foreign company shall have a place of business in Nigeria for any purpose other than the receipt of notice and other documents as preliminary to incorporation under the Decree. See **Wema Bank v. Nigerian National Shipping Line Limited (1979) F.R.C.L.R 133.**

1.3.3 **Companies Act 1990.**

The Companies and Allied Matters Act (CAMA) 1990 was passed into law and commenced on January 2, 1990. An act to establish the Corporate Affairs Commission which provides for the incorporation of companies and incidental matters, the registration of business names, and the incorporation of trustees of certain committees, bodies, and associations.

The 1990 CAMA has 3 parts with 613 sections:

Part A: The establishment of the Corporate Affairs Commission and
Companies

Part B: On business names,

Part C: On Incorporated Trustees and Their Short Title/Schedules

The 1990 Act brought apex remedies and relief to corporate practice. It detailed the arrangement, addition of relative sections, and removal of deterred parts.

1.3.4   COMPANIES AND ALLIED MATTERS ACTS 2004

The 2004 Nigeria Companies and Allied Matters Act (CAMA) was divided into 3 Parts including Part D the short title. The Act placed restrictions on the limited number of persons that can form a company.

Section 18 of CAMA 2004 provides that any two or more persons may form or incorporate a company.

Great similarities exist between the Companies and Allied Matters Act of 1990, 2004, and 2010, with discrepancies in the evolution of light repeals.

1.3.5   THE COMPANIES AND ALLIED MATTERS ACT 2020 AS AMENDED

Sequel to changes in technologies, the electronic operation of transactions, the need for faster and disposed of applications, and approval of consent of the Attorney General in the case of incorporated trustee and company limited by guarantee.

On March 10, 2020, the Senate passed the Companies and Allied Matters Act (CAMA), 2004 (Repeal and Re-enactment) Bill 2018 (the Bill) into law.

The bill divided into eight (8) functions to deal with:

     a. Deals with the administrative aspect of the corporate affairs commission
     b. Deals with the incorporation of companies in Nigeria and incidental matters.
     c. Deals with a limited liability partnership.
     d. Deals with a limited partnership
     e. Deals with business names
     f. Deals with incorporated trustees (non-profit organizations).
     g. Deals with the establishment of an administrative proceedings committee (general).
     h. Provides the short title of the bill.

And would become an act upon being asserted by the president of the Federal Republic of Nigeria.

1.4 FEATURES OF THE COMPANIES AND ALLIED MATTERS ACTS OF 2020 AS AMENDED

a. The Companies and Allied Matters Act 2020 is divided into seven parts. A: Corporate Affairs Commission, B: Incorporation of Companies and Incidental matters, C: The limited liability partnership, D: The limited partnership, E: Business name, Part F incorporated Trustees, and G. General.

b. It provides the Corporate Affairs Commission Board: The establishment of the body (Board of the CAC) which is charged with administering the Act now has representatives of the Institute of Chartered Secretaries and Administrative of Nigeria and the Nigerian Association of Small and Medium Enterprises Section 2(b) iv & v of the Companies and Allied Matters Act. 2020

c. Sole company incorporation: Unlike the rule of formation to be with a minimum of two persons, a single person can now set up a private company, being the director and shareholder. **Section 18(2)**.[9]

d. **Section 26 (12)** provides that the total liability of a member of a company limited by guarantee to contribute to the assets of the company in the event of winding up shall not be less than N100,000 as opposed to N10,000.

e. The electronic application for filing the consent of the Attorney General of the Federation in respect of an incorporated trustee and company limited by guarantee.

f. Increase in the minimum share capital for a private and public company from N10,000.00 to N100,000.00 and N500,000.00 to N2,000,000.00, respectively.[10]

---

[9] Companies and Allied matters Act. Cap. C 20 Laws of the Federation of Nigeria 2020.
[10] Companies and Allied matters Act. Cap. C 20 Laws of the Federation of Nigeria 2020, Section 27 sub 2(a).

g. **Section 31(2)** The commission may, at any time before a certificate of incorporation is issued, withdraw or cancel a reserved name if it discovers that such name is identical to that by which a company in existence is already registered or so nearly resembles it as to be likely to deceive.

h. Power to withdraw, cancel, or revoke a certificate of incorporation that is discovered to be fraudulent, unlawful, or improperly procured. **Section 41 (7) CAMA**.

i. Enclosure of Directors Information as contained in the Register of Directors. **Section 323 of the CAMA 2020**.

j. Provision of a "statement of compliance" against the statutory declaration of compliance to be complied with by the legal practitioner who incorporated the company. **Section 40 CAMA 2020.**

k. Provision of easy electronic signatures for authentication.[11]

l. Exemption of small companies' **Section 237 CAMA 2020** and companies that have shareholders from the mandatory requirement of the Annual General Meeting.

m. **Section 330 (1):** Except in the case of a small company, every company shall have a secretary.

n. Mandates public companies to display their audited accounts on the websites for public accessibility.[12]

o. Provision for any person, foreigners, and inclusive or association of persons to carry on business in Nigeria as a Company, LLP, or business name.

p. Provides electronic transfers of shares.[13]

q. Provides for the establishment of a committee called "the Administrative Committee".

r. Provides that a person shall not be a director in more than five (5) public limited liability companies.[14]ETC

---

[11] Companies and Allied matters Act. Cap. C 20 Laws of the Federation of Nigeria 2020, Section 101.

[12] Ibid., Section 374 (6).

[13] Ibid., Section 175 (1)

[14] Section 307 (1)

CHAPTER 2.

PERSONS ENTITLED TO CARRY OUT INCORPORATION ACTIVITES.

There are categories of persons that can carry out incorporation activities. These persons may be a lawyer or non-lawyer. Essentially the two groups of persons that can carry out incorporation activities are accredited and non-accredited agents. Persons who fall under accredited agents include Nigerian Bar Association Individual, Law Firm, Institute Of Chartered Accountants Of Nigeria Individual, Institute Of Chartered Accountants Of Nigeria Firm, Association Of National Accountants Of Nigeria Individual, Association Of National Accountants Of Nigeria Individual, Association Of National Accountants Of Nigeria Firm, The Institute Of Chartered Secretaries And Administrators Of Nigeria Individual And The Institute Of Chartered Secretaries And Administrators Of Nigeria Firm. While non-accredited agent comprises any individual; lawyer, non-lawyer, or any member of the abovementioned bodies who has no account with the Corporate Affairs Commission.

2.1   ACCREDITED AND NON-ACCREDITED AGENT'S ACCOUNT.

An accredited agent account is an agent's account certified by the Corporate Affairs Commission to process and submit every pre-incorporation registration and post-incorporation filing on behalf of individuals and businesses.

Unlike an accredited agent's account, a non-accredited agent's account is a non-certified user account that is used for single incorporation, having the user as the proprietor or director of the prospect registration. Not every pre-incorporation activity can be carried out in the latter.

2.2   <u>PRACTICAL STEP TO CREATING AN ACCREDITED AGENT ACCOUNT</u>

Step 1: **Enter on your browse-------------------pre.cac.gov.ng**

The below dashboard will be displayed.

HELP OBJECTION FOR IT AND TD/GTE FAQS CONTACT US

Register   Login

Log in to your Account.

Username   Email   Phone Number   Accreditation Number

Enter Username

Submit

New to us? **Sign up**

Click the button below to resend the account verification email.

Resend Email

Step 2;   **Click on <u>Sign up.</u>**

Any member of the public can create an account, kindly note you will be a director, trustee, or proprietor/partner during the registration process. Please provide the necessary details.

Continue Existing/Queried Registration

Please select to create an account as a non-Nigerian.

NIN Details

Phone number

+234 ___________________________________

OR

NIN

12345678912

LOGIN   NEXT

Step 3.   **Enter your phone number or fill in the Eleven-digit NIN and click on next.**

Any member of the public can create an account, kindly note you will be a director, trustee, or proprietor/partner during the registration process. Please provide the necessary details.

_____ Continue Existing/Queried Registration

_____ Please select to create an account as a non-Nigerian.

__※__ **Please select if you want to be an accredited agent.**

Authorized Representative

Surname	First name	Other name

Date of Birth	Gender	Nationality

Account Details

Phone Number	Email	Confirm Email

Username	Password	Confirm Password

Occupation/Description

Address

Country	State	LGA

Post Code	City/Town/Village	House NO/Building Name

Street name

Means of Identification

Type   National Identification Number

Back	Register

Step 4.   Select the option "Please select if you want to be an accredited agent".

Please note that the Corporate Affairs Commission (CAC) has the right to disapprove requests for the accredited user(s) that do not meet all requirements

Step 4(1) **Select Accredited Agent Type.**

1. Create Account	2. Document	3. Payment	4. Confirmation

Accredited Agent Type

Nigerian Bar Association Individual

Authorized Representative

Name	Surname	Other Name

Date of Birth	Gender	Nationality

Account Details

Phone Number	Email	Confirm Email

Username	Password	Confirm Password

Occupation/Description

<u>Address</u>

Country	State	LGA

Post Code	City/Town/Village	House No/Building Name

Street name

<u>Means of Identification</u>

Type :

National ID Card	National Identification Number: 12345678987
Back	**Save & continue**

Note// Select the type of accredited agent fitting to your line of specialty and fill in the other columns, especially your username and password. As an individual legal practitioner, select Nigeria Bar Association Individual. Save and continue at the end of this stage.

Note: upon successful completion of the user registration, the username and password provided herein serve as details for the user's login.

Step 4 (2): **UPLOAD DOCUMENT**

Document	File format	Is requested	Upload	Status	Action

Signature	JPEG/PNG IMAGE	YES	Upload		
A passport Photograph	JPEG/PNG IMAGE	YES	Upload		
Evidence of identification	PDF	YES	Upload		
Qualifying Certificate	PDF	YES	Upload		
NYSC Discharge Certificate/Exemption Letter	PDF	OPTIONAL	Upload		
Current Practicing Fee Receipt	PDF	YES	Upload		
Others	PDF	OPTIONAL	Upload		

Save   **Save & Continue**

Adherence to the format of documents requested and successful uploading of the same saves you against query. Click save & continue.

Step 4 (3): **Payment**

1. Create Account	2. Document	3. **Payment**	4. Confirmation

Please note that you will not be allowed to make modifications after attempting payment

Remitta RRR:123456789123

N10,000.00

Remita	
Description	Amount
Accreditation portal user registration for Individual	N10,166.13

Pay via Remita

BACK

Note: Payment can be made using any of these; ATM Card, bank account, Bank Branch, USSD, QR Code, Internet Banking, Buy on Credit, Wallet, Phone Number, or Bank Transfer

Furthermore, clicking the remita above will direct you to several options for payment. Having selected the mode of payment most convenient to your service and payment of same, the user is redirected to the preview page to download the receipt of payment. Furthermore, an account verification mail would be sent to the user.

Step 4(4):   **Account Verification**

Open the email and click on the link to complete the registration.

Corporate Affairs Commission (CAC)

Thank you, Peace Abah,

You are almost there click here to complete.

Note: All accredited agent applicants are expected to complete the submission of the required document and make the necessary application fee for approval consideration.

Yours faithfully,

Corporate Affairs Commission

Note: On successful verification of the Email and account, the Approving officer approves the application, and a further mail will be sent to the user having the accreditation number. Return to the portal and log in using the username and password selected during the creation of the account. Furthermore, users can log in using any of their choices; username, email, accredited number, or phone number.

Chapter 3.

INCORPORATION

Incorporation is the process of formation, registration, and setting up of a legal entity be it sole proprietor, company, or incorporated trustee. It is the registration of every entity profit or not-for-profit entity with the Corporate Affairs Commission. Upon incorporation, the registered entity becomes a body corporate [15] by the name described in the certificate with perpetual succession, a common seal, and the power to sue and be sued under such a corporate name. [16]

Benefit of Incorporation[17]

- They become a body corporate capable of owning property see the case of **AKUNMWATA JOE OGUEJIOFOR ANYAEGBUNAM V. PASTOR OKWUDILI OSAKA & ORS[18]** where the court held that the gift of the said property to the non-existent Light of Christ Praying Band is ineffectual, null and void and of no effect whatsoever.
- Enjoy perpetual succession.
- Sue and be sued in the incorporated name.
- Do and suffer such other acts and things as bodies corporate may lawfully do and suffer.

3.1   **Pre-incorporation**

This entails the resolution of ideas, steps, plans toward the birthing of any legal entity. It is the stage-by-stage process before the incorporation of a company. This activity includes pre-incorporation contracts, securing premises, fundraising, registration be that as a business name (sole proprietor or partnership), company, profit, or not-for-profit association.

---

[15] Section 42. CAMA 2020 as Amended.

[16] Akunwata Joe Oguejiofor Anyaegbunam V. Pastor Okwudili Osaka & Ors (2000) LLJR-SC

[17] Section 42. Ibid.

[18] (2000)LLJR-SC

Pre-incorporation of a business name, company or incorporated trustee commences with logging into a CAC account which could be an accredited account or a non-accredited account. Conduct an availability name search and reservation. This is to avoid the use of the same name or closely related name of an existing company.

3.1.2 Availability Names Search and Reservation of Names

Carrying out a name search is important before reservation of the said name. A search could be conducted word-for-word with the prospective business name or by simply pasting the prospective name in the search box.

Restricted and Prohibited Names[19]

Section 852. No company, limited liability partnership, limited partnership, business name, or incorporated trustee shall be registered under this Act by a name or trademark which—

(a) is identical with that by which a company or limited liability partnership in existence is already registered, or so nearly resembles that name as to be calculated to deceive, except where the company or limited liability partnership in existence is in the course of being dissolved and signifies its consent in such manner as the Commission requires ;

(b) contains the words "Chamber of Commerce" unless it is a company limited by guarantee;

(c) in the opinion of the Commission, is capable of misleading as to the

---

[19] Section 852. CAMA 2020 as amended.

nature or extent of its activities or is undesirable, offensive, or otherwise contrary to public policy;

(d) in the opinion of the Commission, would violate or conflict with any existing trademark or business name registered in Nigeria or body corporate formed under this Act unless the consent of the owner of the trademark, business name, or trustees of the body corporate has been obtained;

(e) contains any word which, in the opinion of the Commission, is likely to mislead the public as to the nationality, race, or religion of the persons by whom the business is wholly or mainly owned or controlled;

(f) is, in the opinion of the Commission, deceptive or objectionable in that it contains a reference or suggests an association with any practice, institution, personage, foreign state or government, international organization or international brand or is otherwise unsuitable; or
(g) is capable of undermining public peace and national security.

(2) Except with the consent of the Commission, no company, limited liability partnership, limited partnership, business name, or incorporated trustees shall be registered by a name which—

(a) includes the word "Federal", "National", "Regional", and "State" ;

(b)   "Government", or any other word which, in the opinion of the Commission suggests or is calculated to suggest that it enjoys the patronage of the Government of the Federation, the Government of a State in Nigeria, any Ministry or Department of Government, or contains the word "Municipal" or "Chartered" or in the opinion of the Commission, suggests or is calculated to suggest, connection with any municipality or other local authority;

(c)   contains the word "Cooperative" or its equivalent in any other language or any abbreviation; or of the words "Building Society"; or

(d) contains the word "Group" or "Holding".

(3)   No individual or firm shall be registered under PART D or E of this Act if the age of the individual or any individual who is a partner is stated in the statement furnished under section 796 of this Act to be less than 18 years unless the statement shows at least two other individuals aged above 18 years.

(4)   No company, business name, or incorporated trustee shall be registered where there is irrefutable evidence to the effect that the company, business name, or incorporated trustee has previously been involved in fraudulent trade malpractices, either in local or international trade.

N/B: names can still be denied on the grounds of uncertainty, vagueness, and relative meaninglessness. And cases where the nature of the business or its aims and objectives contradict and conflict with the public interest, equity, religion, and good conscience.

3. 1.3   Business Name[20]

"Every individual, firm or Corporation having a place of business in Nigeria and carrying on business under a business name shall be registered in the manner provided in this Part if—

(a)   in the case of a firm, the name does not consist of the true surname of all partners without any addition other than the true forenames of the individual partners or the initials of such forenames;

(b)   in the case of an individual, the name does not consist of his true surname without any addition other than his true forename or the initials thereof; or

(c)   in the case of a company, whether or not registered under this Act, the name does not consist of its corporate name without any addition.

(2) Notwithstanding subsection (1) where —

---

[20] Section 815(1) to (4) CAMA 2020 as Amended

(a)   the addition merely indicates that the business is carried on in succession to a former owner of the business, that addition shall not of itself render registration necessary;

(b)   two or more individual partners have the same surname, the addition of an "s" at the end of that surname shall not of itself render registration necessary; and

(c)   the business is carried on by a receiver or manager appointed by any court, registration shall not be necessary.

815. (1) Every individual, firm, or company required under this Act to be registered shall, within 28 days after the individual, firm, or corporation

commences the business in respect of which registration is required, furnish to the Registrar at the registry in the State in which the principal place of business of the individual, firm or company is situated, a statement in writing in the prescribed

form, signed as required by this section and containing the following particulars—

(a) the business name or, if the business is carried on under two or more business names, each of those business names;

(b) the general nature of the business;

(c) the full postal address of the principal place of business;

(d) the full postal address of every other place of business;

(e) where the registration to be effected is that of a firm:

(i)   the present forenames and surname, any former forenames or surname, the nationality and, if that nationality is not the nationality of origin, the nationality of origin, the age, the sex, the usual residence, and any other business occupation of each of the individuals who are partners; and

(ii) the corporate name and registered office of such company which is a partner ;

(f) where the registration to be effected is that of an individual, the present forenames and surname, any former forenames or surnames, the nationality and, if that nationality is not the nationality of origin, the nationality of origin, the age, the sex, the usual residence and any other business occupation of the individual;

(g) where the registration to be effected is that of a company, the name and registered office of the company ; and

(h) the date of commencement of the business, whether before or after the coming into operation of this Act.

(2)   Where the registration to be effected is that of an individual or a firm, some or all of whose partners are individuals, there shall be submitted to the Registrar copies

of the passport photographs of the individual certified in a manner required by the Registrar.

(3)   Where the registration to be effected is that of a firm or individual carrying on business on behalf of another individual, firm, or corporation whether as nominee or trustee, the statement required by subsection (1) to be furnished shall contain the

  following particulars in addition to the particulars required by that subsection—

(a)   the present forenames and surname, any former forenames or surname, the nationality and, if that nationality is not the nationality of origin, the nationality of origin and the usual residence of each individual on whose behalf the business is carried on; and

(b)   the name of each firm or corporation on whose behalf the business is carried on.

(4)   Where the registration to be effected is that of a firm or individual carrying on business as general agent for any concern carrying on business outside Nigeria and not having a place of business in Nigeria, the statement required by subsection (1) to be furnished shall, in addition to the particulars required by that subsection, state the name and full postal address of each such concern, provided that in the case of a firm or individual carrying on business as general agent for three or more such concerns, it shall be sufficient to state the fact that the business is so carried on and the countries in which the concerns carry on business".

Business Name comprises Firm, Enterprise, Ventures, Multi-Ventures etc

3. 1. 4   **Reservation and Registration of Business Names.**

Business name reservation and registration are broken down into two parts,

Part 1. Name reservation of two proposed names.

   a) Objectives of the name reservation/reason for availability search.
   b) Preview and payment.
   c) Once reserved, click on the reserved name and commence registration.

   Part 2. Registration of business name

a) Entity description, date of commencement/contact address, and email/ address of the business.
b) Nature of the business.
c) Proprietor's Details.
d) Documents needed for upload include a National Identity Card, the signature of the proprietor, and passport photography.

Practice; Enter on your browse-------------------pre.cac.gov.ng.

HELP OBJECTION FOR IT AND LTD/GTE FAQS CONTACT US

Register   Login

Log in to your Account

Username   Email   Phone Number   Accreditation number

Enter Username

Submit

New to us? Sign up

Click the button below to resend the account verification email

Resend Email

>>>>Enter username and submit.

HELP OBJECTION FOR IT AND LTD/GTE FAQS CONTACT US

Register   Login

Log in to your account

Welcome Back

Enter Password:

Forgot your password click here

Login

New to us? Sign up

Click the button below to resend the account verification email.

Resend Email

\>\>\>\>\>\>\>Enter the user password and log in.

Step a.   Click on   **New Name Reservation**

0	0		
NOT SUBMITTED	PENDING/QUERIED	0 DENIED	0 RESERVED

     ※   **New Name Reservation**.
Registration

NOT SUBMITTED	PENDING APPROVAL	QUERIED	RESERVED

Register a Company/Business Name/Incorporated Trustee Start registration with your Name Availability Click here.

New Company Registration

Step b.   Select the company type and fill in the two proposed names.

1. Name and Type	2. Objectives	3. Preview	4. Payment

Company Type Classification.   Specific Type

Business name	Business Name-Sole Proprietor

Proposed Names

Option 1.

Option 2

DICE GADGETS	DICE ENTERPRISE

Back.   **Save   and   continue.**

******Select the classified you intend to register; Business Name, Company, Incorporated Trustee, Limited Partnership, and Limited Liability Partnership*****

Select a specific Type.

*******Business name-Sole Proprietorship or Business name-Partnership*******

Step c.   **Select the reason for the availability search.**

1.NameandType	2.**Objectives**	3. Preview	4. Payment

Reason for Availability Search.

New Incorporation/Registration

Nature of Business Category

Specific Nature of Business

Other service activities	Other personal services activities

Additional Remarks

Registration

****Reason for name Reservation/pre-incorporation includes change of Name, Group Holdings/Consortium, Name Substitution, New Incorporation/Registration, Registration of Business name as Limited (LTD)****

Step d.   **Preview/Checkmate.**

1.NameandType	2. Objectives	3. **Preview**	4. Payment

Entity Details

Proposed Name (option 1)	DICE GADGETS
Proposed Name (option 2)	DICE ENTERPRISE
Classification	BUSINESS NAME
Company Type	BUSINESS NAME- SOLE PROPRIETOR

Objectives

Reason for Name Availability Search	New Incorporation/Registration
Nature of Business	
Additional Comments	

Presenter Details

Name	Peace Abah
Telephone	08012345678

Email	peaceabah123@gmail.com
Contact Address	Maitama Abuja

Step e. **Payment.**

See pages 21 and 22 for the payment procedure, use the most convenient for your network provider and make the payment.

After payment, the work moves from not submitted to Pending/Queried

Note: Approved Names move to the reserved column while Denied names move to the Denied column. Click on the reserved column and click on start registration which is showing on top of the reserved name and commence the registration.

REGISTRATION OF BUSINESS NAME.

STAGE 1. Click on the Reserved section, and at the top of the reserved name click on Start Registration

0	0	0	1
NOT SUBMITTED	PENDING/QUERIED	DENIED	**RESERVED**

New Name Registration

Registration

Search
___select Status______

APPROVAL HISTORY

Start registration	Approval Note	Download Receipt

DICE ENTERPRISE

Company

Created on Dec 31, 2020	Submitted on Dec 31, 2020	Approved on Dec 31, 2020

BUSINESS DETAILS	PARTICULARS OF PROPRIETORS	NATURE OF BUSINESS	DOCUMENT UPLOAD	PREVIEW	PAYMENT

DICE ENTERPRISE

Business commencement Date

State the exact date you commenced the registration.

Email	Phone number

Principal Place of Business

State	LGA	City/Town/Village

Postcode	House Number/building name

Street name

Branch Address (If any)

Branch State	Branch LGA	Branch City

Branch House Number/Description:		Post Code

Branch Street Name:

Add Branch

Branch Address	Action

Back   Save &Continue

Note: filling of the Branch Address attracts an additional charge of ten thousand naira only.

STAGE 2. **THE PROPRIETOR**

Note: The requisite identity for the individual proprietor is the National Identity Card (NIN), Driver's License, Volter's card, International Passport, etc. while that of the corporate proprietor is the registered number or registered name of the entity.

Click on Add individual proprietor and fill out the form with the provided proprietor's details or click on autofill to fill the form using the NIN.

On successful linking of the NIN, the details of the holder as saved with NIMC uploads. Fill in the remaining parts, such as the address and occupation, where necessary.

In cases of non-citizens, click on the fill form for Foreigners.

On complete filling out the form, click on add proprietor, and click on save and continue. See the diagram below.

BUSINESS NAME

BUSINESS DETAILS	**PARTICULARS OF PROPRIETORS**	NATURE OF BUSINESS	DOCUMENT UPLOAD	PREVIEW	PAYMENT

DICE ENTERPRISE

Add Individual Proprietor	Add Corporate Proprietor	Add minor person

Surname | First Name | Other Name

Date of Birth | Gender | Nationality

Former Name (if any) | Former Nationality (If any)

Phone number | Email

+234

Service Address

Country | State | LGA

City

street

Add Partner

S/N	Name	Telephone	Email	Contact Address	Proprietor type	Action
1	Peace Abah	07012345678	Peaceabah123@gmail.com	NO. 1. Empress plaza, Wuse Amac, FCT, Nigeria	Individual proprietor	Edit Delete

Back   **Save &Continue**

Nature of Business

The following comprises the nature of business to every incorporation.

1. Accommodation and food services activities.
2. Activities of extraterritorial Organizations and bodies.
3. Activities of house of employment undifferentiated Goods-and services producing activities of households for own use.
4. Administrative and support services activities.
5. Art, Entertainment, and Recreation.
6. Agriculture forestry & fishing.
7. Community-based association.
8. Cultural-based association.
9. Construction.

10. Education.

11. Faith-based association.

12. Financial and Insurance Activities.

13. Foundation-based association.

14. Human health and social work activities.

15. Information and communication.

16. Manufacturing.

17. Mining and Quarrying.

18. Other Service Activities.

19. Others.

20. Power.

21. Professional Scientific and Technical Activities.

22. Public administration and Defence; Defence, compulsory social security.

23. Real estate activities.

24. Repairs of motor vehicles and motorcycles.

25. Social Clubs-based association.

26. Sporting-based association.

27. Transportation.

28. Water supply, sewerage, waste management, and remediation activities.

29. Wholesale and retail trade; repair of motor vehicles and motorcycles.

Each of these activities has its specific nature of business.

Kindly select the one that matches the client's business and fill also the description of the said business.

See below.

STAGE 3

DICE ENTERPRISE

BUSINESS DETAILS	PARTICULARS OF PROPRIETORS	**NATURE OF BUSINESS**	DOCUMENT UPLOAD	PREVIEW	PAYMENT

Nature of Business Category   Specific Nature of Business

Other Service Activities	Film Production Services

Other Nature of Business Description.

To carry on the business of Film production, music production, and other artistic displays.

Add the nature of business	Cancel

Nature of Business

s/n	Category	Nature of business	Other description	Action
1	Other Service activities	Film Production services	To carry on the business of film production, music production, and other artistic display	Edit Delete

Back   **Save & Continue**

STAGE 4

BUSINESS NAME

BUSINESS DETAILS	PARTICULARS OF PROPRIETORS	NATURE OF BUSINESS	**DOCUMENT UPLOAD**	PREVIEW	PAYMENT

DICE ENTERPRISE

Document Requirement for Business name

Maximum of 5MB size per document type 1

S/N	DOCUMENT	FILE FORMAT	IS REQUIRED	UPLOAD	STATUS	ACTION
1	Evidence of identification	Pdf	Yes	Upload		
2	Signature	Jpeg/png image	Yes	Upload		
3	A Passport photograph	Jpeg/png	Yes	Upload		
4	Other	Pdf	Optional	Upload		

STAGE 5

BUSINESS DETAILS	PARTICULARS OF PROPRIETORS	NATURE OF BUSINESS	DOCUMENTS UPLOAD	**PREVIEW**	PAYMENT

BUSINESS NAME DETAILS

Classification	Business name

Business Commencement date	January 01, 2021
Address	No 1. Empress Plaza, Wuse, Abuja.
Branch Address	

Nature of Business

S/N	Category	Specific	Description
1	Other service activities	Film production services	To carry on the business of film production, music production, and other artistic display.

Proprietor/ Partner(s)

Name	Peace Abah
Telephone	08123456789
Gender	Female
Date of Birth	April 01, 1996
Contact Address	01 Empress Plaza Wuse, Abuja.
Type	Proprietor

Presenter Details

Name	Peace Abah
Telephone	08012345678
Email	peaceabah123@gmail.com

Contact Address	Maitama Abuja
Date of birth	April 01, 1996
Nationality	Nigeria
Accreditation Number (if any)	NBA/IND/111222
Gender	Female

Back   **Save &Continue**

For the payment procedure, see page 21.

NOTE: Upon approving of the business name, an email will be sent to the user's mail asking them to please log in to view/download your certificate…" It's advisable to log in and download all the approved documents (the certificate and the status report) within the seven (7) days grace of its approval. Downloading not within the free days attract a charge of #5,000, per document. This applies to all pre-incorporation approved work.

3.1.5   **Company.**

A Company is a registered entity, or business arrangement that enjoys a legal personality separate from its members. Companies are divided into two kinds: Private company and public company, which are in turn subdivided into six (6) types.

Private Company Limited by Shares, Private Unlimited Company, Private Company Limited by Guarantee, Public Company Limited by Shares, Public Unlimited Company, and Public Company Limited by Guarantee

Where a company has the liability of its members limited by the memorandum to the amount, if any, unpaid on the shares respectively held by them, such a company is limited by shares or Having the liability of its members limited by the memorandum to such amount as the members may respectively thereby undertake to contribute to the assets of the company in the event of its being wound up, such a company is limited by guarantee or

Not having any limit on the liability of its members (an unlimited company).[21]

3.1.6 RESERVATION OF NAMES FOR COMPANY REGISTRATION

Step 1.   Click on the new Name Reservation

0	0	0	0
NOT SUBMITTED	PENDING/QUERIED	DENIED	RESERVED

※   **New Name Reservation**.

Registration

NOT SUBMITTED	PENDING APPROVAL	QUERIED	RESERVED

a. From the dashboard Click on **new name reservation** this will take you to the dashboard below, select the company type, and fill in the two proposed names.

1. **Name and Type**	2. Objectives	3. Preview	4. Payment

---

[21] Section 21 (1) and (2) companies and Allied Matters Act 2020, as Amended. C 20. Laws of the Federal republic of Nigeria.

Company Type

Classification.   Specific Type

Company	Private Company Limited by Shares

Proposed Names

Option 1.

Option 2

CEA Nigeria Ltd	ADIS Nigeria Ltd

Back.   **Save and continue.**

******Select the classified you intend to register; Business Name, Company, Incorporated Trustee, Limited Partnership, and Limited Liability Partnership*****

Select a specific Type.

********Private Company limited by Shares*******

Note: Other types include Private Unlimited Company, Public Company Limited by Shares, Public Unlimited Company, Private Company Limited by Guarantee, and Public Company Limited by Guarantee.

*******Enter the proposed name in option one and two, attention to be given to the specific word end "LTD or Limited"*********.

Step b.   **Select the reason for the availability search.**

1. Name and Type	2. **Objectives**	3. Preview	4. Payment

Reason for the Availability Search.

New Incorporation/Registration

Additional Remarks

Registration

****Reasons for name Reservation/pre-incorporation includes change of Name, Group Holdings/Consortium, Name Substitution, New Incorporation/Registration, Registration of Business name as Limited (LTD)****

Step c.   **Preview/Checkmate.**

1. Name and Type	2. Objectives	3. **Preview**	4. Payment

Entity Details

Proposed Name (option 1)	CEA NIGERIA LTD
Proposed Name (option 2)	ADIS NIGERIA LTD
Classification	Company
Company Type	Private Company limited by Shares

Objectives

Reason for Name Availability Search:	New Incorporation/Registration
Additional Comments	

Presenter Details

Name	Peace Abah

Telephone	08012345678
Email	peaceabah123@gmail.com
Contact Address	Maitaima Abuja

Back   **Save and Continue**

Step d.   Payment.

See page 21 for the payment procedure, use the most convenient for you.

After payment, it moves from not submitted to Pending/Queried

Note: Approved Names move to the reserved column while Denied names move to the Denied column.

3.1.7   **Procedural Registration of a Private Company Limited by Shares**

Step 1. Click on the reserved icon and click on Start Registration on the top of the approved name.

Name Reservation

0	0	0	1
NOT SUBMITTED	PENDING/QUERIED	DENIED	RESERVED

New Name Registration

Registration

NOT SUBMITTED	PENDING APPROVAL	QUERIED	APPROVED

Click on start registration as shown to you below

Search
____select Status________

APPROVAL HISTORY

Start registration	Approval Note	Download Receipt

CEA NIGERIA LTD Company

Created on April 01, 2023	Submitted on April 01, 2023	Approved on April 01, 2023

Step 2.   **(Registration)**

The steps for registration of a company are broken down into 11 sub-steps from A to K which include:

a. Entity Details

b. Objects of the Memorandum

c. Articles of Association

d. Directors

e. Secretary

f. Statement of issued share capital.

g. Persons with significant control (PSC)

h. Statement of Compliance

i. Document upload

j. Preview and

k. Payment

Step 2. (a)   **Entity Details of the Company**

- Fill in the details as stated, starting with the principal business activity classifications 1 and 2. Select the exact business activity that match the client's business plan.
- The Principal Activity Description should be clear and straight without any invited symbols.
- Email and phone number.
- The registered address and head office address (if different from the registered address) should be easily traceable and situated in Nigeria.
- Branch Address: Filling a branch address attracts an additional fee of ten thousand naira only.

See the diagram below.

CEA NIGERIA LTD

Principal Business Activity Classification 1	Principal Business Activity Classification 2

Principal Activity Description

Email

Phone Number

Registered Address

State   LGA   City/Town/Village

Post Code   House Number/Building Name

Street Name

Head Office Address (If different from Registered Office)

Country   State   LGA

City/Town/Village   Post Code   House NO/Building Name

Street Name

Back   **Save & Continue**.

N/B. CLICK save and continue at the end of any page.

Step 2. (b)   **Objects of the Memorandum**.

- At least one objective should be added.
- All the objectives of the business should be added one after the other and not as one object for all.
- Upon adding any objective, click Add at the end of the column and add another objective. (one after the other)
- Save and continue to proceed to the next page.

See the diagram below!

CEA NIGERIA LTD

Object*

Add | Cancel

Back   **Save &Continue**

Step 2. (c); Article of Association.

- Details of the Articles of Association comprises the witness; the power and responsibilities of the directors; shares and distributions; dividends and other distributions; capitalization of profits, the power, and responsibilities of shareholders; voting; administrative arrangements, directors' indemnity and insurance.

- The witness: By CAC Regulation 2022/2023. The prescribed document for filing any legal (human) detail is the National Identity Card for Nigerians. However, a foreigner can be the witness of a company having his country's identity card which will be uploaded in document section. Note: The witness shall be a separate body from the director and shareholder.

- Adopt the default Articles of Association therein provided. This enables fast incorporation and ease drafting procedures. Adopt same for a company that has no articles.

- Save and continue.

SEE THE DIAGRAM BELOW.

CEA NIGERIA LTD

Auto-fill form with NIN	Fill Form for Foreigner

ARTICLES OF ASSOCIATION-WITNESS INFORMATION

Surname	First Name	Other Name

Contact Details

Occupation/Description	Email

Phone number

+234

Service Address

Country	State	LGA

Date of Birth	Gender	Nationality

Post Code	City/Town/Village	House No/Building Name

Street Name

[   ]

[Add Another Witness   ]

witness

S/N	Name	Telephone	Email	Contact Address	Action
1	Joy Peters	07012345678	joypeters@gmail.com	101/A, Fine villa Maitama, Amac, FCT, Nigeria	Edit Delete

Add Articles	**Adopt Default Articles**

Back   **Save and Continue**

Step 2. (d)   Directors

- A minimum of one director is needed to proceed with the registration of a private company, while public companies must have a minimum of two directors.
- For Nigerians, a national identity card (NIN) is a great requisite, as no Nigerian can be appointed as a director with other cards like a permanent voter's card, a national driver's license, an age declaration, a birth certificate, or an international passport unless the NIN restriction is lifted.
- Provision of a service address, which may be different from the residential address. If both are the same click on Use Service Address as Residential Address.
- Hide of the residential address attracts a cost of N25,000.00, payable along with the registration charge.

- A small company can have a single person as the director, secretary, and shareholder. A small company can waive the role of secretary. The option of making a director the shareholder is indicated to ease registration assignment.
- In the case of a foreign director, other means of identification could be applicable.
- Kindly click on Add another director, to down-fill the director, and click save and control thereafter. You can repeat the process to add more directors.
- See the diagram below.

Add Director	Autofill Form with NIN	Fill Form For Foreigner's

Personal Details

Surname   First Name   Other Name

Date of Birth   Gender   Nationality

Former Name (if any)   Former Nationality (If any)

Contact Details

Phone number

+234   Email   Occupation

Service Address

This is the address that will appear on the public record. This does not have to be your usual residential address. Please state 'The Company's Registered Office' if your service address will be recorded in the proposed company's register of directors as the company's registered office.

Country	State	LGA

Post Code	City/Town/Village	House Number/Building Name

street

- **Use Service Address as Residential Address**

Residential Address

Please state 'Same as service address' in this section if your usual residential address is recorded in the company's proposed register of director's residential addresses as 'Same as service address'. You cannot state 'Same as service address' if your service address has been stated above as 'The Company's Registered Office'. You will need to complete the address in full.

Country	State	LGA

Post Code	City/Town/Village	House Number/Building Name

street

- **Hide Residential Address From Public Records?**

This service attracts an additional fee of N25,000

- **Make Director Shareholder?**

Means of Identification

Type	Identity Number

DIRECTOR(S)

S/N	Name	Telephone	Email	Contact Address	Action
1	Peace Abah	07012345678	Peaceabah123@gmail.com	101/A, Fine villa Maitama, Amac, FCT, Nigeria	Edit Delete

Back   **Save & Continue**

Step 2 (e)   Secretary

- The appointment of a secretary is optional for small companies unlike that of public companies. You may click on the option displayed to skip the stage.
- A secretary can either be an individual (A Nigerian citizen or foreigner) or a corporate secretary (a juristic person).
- For an individual, fill in the detailed information prescribed.
- For a corporate secretary, click on Add corporate secretary; search for the company using its registered name or registration number.
- The address of the corporate secretary must be a physical location and not a PO Box number. (Use the head office address of the corporate secretary.)
- Means of identification for corporate secretary/director is the company certificate.
- For corporate secretary, click on the displayed name upon typing the registered name or number and complete other fields. For individual secretary click on "Add individual secretary" and fill out the form.

- Save and continue.

See the form below for a corporate secretary.

Add individual secretary	**Add Corporate Secretary**
Autofill Form with NIN	Fill Form For Foreigner's

Entity Details

Search by Company Name/Registration number/Availability Code

1234567

Sewala Venture LTD {1234567}

Company Name	Registration Number
Sewala Venture LTD	RC 1234567

Contact Details

Phone Number	Email

Registered or Principal Address

Country	State	LGA

Post Code	City/Town/Village	House No/Building Name

Street Name

Back   **Save and Continue**

Share Capital Designated to Companies.

Step 2(f)   Statement of Issued Share Capital
  • Minimum Share Capital for designated companies

SN	TYPE OF COMPANY	MINIMUM SHARECAPITAL (N)	JUSTIFICATION
1	Issuing House	200 Million	
2	Broker/Dealer	300 Million	
3	Trustee	300 Million	
4	Fund/Portfolio Manager	150 Million	
5	Stock Broker	200 Million	Securities and Exchange Commission. Guidelines on new minimum share capital for market operators.
6	Stock Dealer	100 Million	
7	Corporate Investment Adviser (Registrar)	150 Million	
8	Corporate investment Adviser	5 Million	
9	Individual Investment Adviser	2 Million	
10	Market Maker	2 Billion	
11	Consultant (Partnership)	2 million	
12	Consultant (individual)	500,000	
13	Consultant (Corporate)	5 million	
14	Underwriter	200 million	CBN Scope and Standards Commercial Regulations 2020
15	Venture capital manager	20 million	,, ,,
16	Commodities broker	40 million	
17	Capital trade point	20 million	
18	Rating Agency	150 million	

19	Corporate/ sub Broker	5 million	
20	Asset management (intangible assets)	300 million	CBN Scope and Standards Commercial Regulations 2020
21	Commercial bank with a regional authorization	10 billion	
22	Commercial bank with national Authorization	25 billion	
23	Commercial bank with international Authorization	50 billion	
24	Merchant bank	15 billion	CBN Scope, Condition, and Minimum Standard for Merchant Bank Regulation 2, 2010.
25	Payment solution services (PSS) (as permissible under super agent, PTS, and PSSP (combined)	250 million	
26	Super Agent (Agent recruitment management under activities as specified in the Regulatory framework for licensing super agents in Nigeria	50 Million	
27	Payment Terminal Service Provider (PTSP) (POS Terminal Deployment and Services, POS terminal Ownership, PTAD, Merchant Service Aggregation and Collection)	100 Million	CBN Guidelines on licensing framework/Categorization for the Nigerian Payment system 2020
28	Payment solution service provider (PSSP) (Payment processing gateway and portal, payment solution/ application development, merchant service Aggregation and collection.	100 million	

No.	Institution	Capital	Regulation
29	Mobile Money operation (E Money issuing, wallet creation and management, pool account management activities as permissible under super agent)	2 billion	CBN Guidelines on licensing framework/Categorization for the Nigerian Payment system 2020
30	Switching and Processing (Switching Card Processing Transaction, Clearing and Settlement agent services, Non-Bank Acquiring services activities as permissible under Super Agent, PTSP, and PSSP)	2 billion	
31	Unit Micro Finance Bank (Tier 1)	Tier 1:200 million	CBN Regulation
32	Unit Micro Finance Bank (Tier 2)	Tier 2:50 million	
33	Micro Finance Bank (state & FCT)	1 billion	
34	Micro Finance Bank (National)	5 billion	
35	Primary Mortgage Institution	2 billion	
36	Finance Company	20 million	
37	Bureau De Change	35 million	
38	Non-Interest Bank (Regional)	5 billion	
39	Non-Interest Bank (National)	10 billion	
40	Insurance Broker	5 million	Nigerian Council of Regulation Insurance Brokers Act 2003
41	Life Insurance	8 billion	National Insurance Commission Revised Regulation 2019
42	General Insurance	10 billion	
43	Composite Insurance	18 billion	
44	Re-Insurance	20 billion	

45	Unit Micro insurer	40 million	Guidelines for Micro-Insurance Operation in Nigeria 2018
46	State Micro insurer	100 million	,, ,,
47	National Micro insurer	600 million	,, ,,
48	Takaful Insurance (General and Family Takaful)	200 million	National Insurance Commission Regulations
49	Private Security company/ consultant	10 million	Guidelines on Requirements for Registration of Private Guards Security companies made under Nigerian Security and Civil Defence Corp Act. No. 2 of 2003
50	Pension Fund/Asset Custodian	2 billion	National Pensions Commission Requirements for licensing of pension fund custodians (Feb. 2015); National Pensions commission Revised Minimum Share Capital Requirements for licensed Pension Fund Administrations (April 2021)
51	Closed pension Fund	500 million	
52	Pension Fund Administrator	5 billion	
53	Lottery	5 million	Section 2 (1), National Lotteries (Amendment) Regulation, 2007
54	Sports Lottery	30 million	National Lottery Commission Circular
55	Air transport (International)	2 billion	
56	Air transport (Regional)	1 billion	
57	Air transport (local)	500 million	Nigerian Civil Aviation Authority
58	Air Ambulance/ Fumigation/ Private jet	20 million	
59	Aviation (ground handling services)	500 million	

60	Aviation (Air Transport Training institution)	2 million	
61	Agents of Foreign Airlines	1 million	
62	Travel/Tours	30 million	International Air Travel Agency (IATA)
63	Agricultural Seeds, Production, Processing, Marketing.	10 million	NASA Cap 5. LFN 2004
64	Shipping Company/Agent	25 million	NIMASA Cap 5 LFN, 2004
65	Cabotage trade	25 million	
66	Life Micro-insurance	150 million	Guidelines for micro- Finance Operation in Nigeria (NAICOM) December 2013
67	General micro-insurance	200 million	,, ,, ,,
68	Freight forwarding	5 million	Regulation of Freight Forwarding Regulation 2010
69	Payment service bank	5 billion	
70	Health maintenance organization (HMO)(National)	400 million (paid up)	National Health insurance Scheme HMO accreditation Guidelines
71	Health Maintenance Organization (HMO)(Regional)	200 million (paid up)	
72	Health Maintenance Organization (HMO) (State)	100 million (paid up)	

With the above analysis, one is familiar with the ratio of shares assigned to a specific company. Click on **Close** beneath the list.

In the prescribed form.

a. Start by selecting the type of the company, this automatically provides the minimum share capital of that company.

b. Type the total company-issued share capital.

c. The breakdown of total issued share capital, the class of shares preference or equity (ordinary).

d. Division into (number of units) least number is 2. Note: In the instance of a sole shareholder, Divide the shares by the total issued share capital. While for two shareholders or more still divide with the total issued share capital.

e. On successful filling of the above, click on Add Share details.

f. A shareholder can either be an individual or a corporate shareholder.

g. Within the filing of the director, an option to make director shareholder has been indicated. If such was clicked, you only need to click on edit beside the shareholder's name and allot shares to the person. Otherwise, click on Add Shareholder which could be an individual shareholder, corporate shareholder, minor shareholder, or foreigner, Note: On the ground of a minor shareholder, the NIN of the minor` is still needed.

h. Attention is given to share allotment as the total shares should be completely allotted.

i. Select the prescribed particulars of right owned by the shareholder, which option c, seems preferable, thus particulars of any rights as respecting capital, to participate in a distribution (including on winding up).

j. Click on Add shareholder upon compliance with the above.

k. Save and continue to proceed to the next stage.

Diagram of the statement of issued share capital.

1. Total company-issued share capital

Type of Company	Minimum Share Capital
Entity with shares below five million	100,000

Total issued share capital	Total issued share capital in words.
1,000,000.00	0ne million naira

Share Details

Breakdown of total company-issued share capital

Class of Shares

Equity (Ordinary) share

Divided into (Number of Units)	Nominal value of each share (Price per unit)
1,000,000.00	# 1

Add share details. Company shares details

S/N	Class of shares	Issued share capital	Issued share capital in words	Divided into (number of units)	Nominal value of each share (price per unit)	Action
1	Equity (Ordinary)shares	1,000,000.00	One million naira	1,000,000.00	1	Edit Delete

Add shareholders.

Add individual shareholders.

Add Corporate shareholder   Add minor shareholder.

S/N	Name	Telephone	Email	Shares allotted	Shareholder type	Aggregate nominal value	Action
1	Peace Abah	07012345678	Peaceabah123@gmail.com	1,000,000 Equity (ordinary) shares	Individual Shareholder	1,000,000	Edit delete

Back   **save/Continue.**

Step 2. (g).   **Person of significant control (PSC)**

- A PSC can either be a natural person or a legal entity.
- On a default, the shareholder details will be updated to that of the PSC under natural person.
- If otherwise, fill in the details by following the format stated therein.
- Note on interest (s) and the percentage held. A sole shareholder must hold 100% in the parts of direct share or interest/voting rights and 0 percent indirectly.
- In the case of two or more shareholders, which will automatically reflect as Persons of Significant Control (PSC), the percentage taken in shares should be equal to the percent of control to be given to the PSC.
- Further note that instances of inappropriate PSC percentage control will amount to a query. Example: where two shareholders happen to be allotted shares of one million with the ratio of seven hundred thousand shares to A and three hundred thousand shares to B, this implies that A will hold 70% in the PSC and B will hold 30%.
- Yes, to be answered on the grounds of whether the PSC holds directly or indirectly and can relate to the question asked. And No, to be answered where the PSC does not have those rights or capacity. This should be properly answered. Click on Save and continue. •

See the diagram below.

<u>Diagram of Person with Significant Control</u>

CEA NIGERIA LIMITED

A person with significant control (PSC)" means the natural person(s) who ultimately owns or controls a company or limited liability partnership or the natural person on whose behalf a transaction is being conducted and includes those natural persons who exercise ultimate effective control over a legal person or arrangement. To qualify as a PSC, the person must meet any of the following conditions in relation to a company or limited liability partnership

- Holds at least 5% of the issued shares in a company or interest in a limited liability partnership either directly or indirectly,

- Exercises at least 5% of the voting rights in a company or limited liability partnership directly or indirectly;
- Holds a right directly or indirectly, to appoint or remove a majority of the directors of the company or partners of the limited liability.
- Exercises significant influence or control, directly or indirectly, over the company or limited liability partnership; or
- Having the right to exercise, or exercise significant influence or control over the activities of a trust or firm, whether or not it is a legal entity, would satisfy any of the first four conditions if it were an individual.
- NOTE: being a shareholder qualifies the person to be a person with significant control. Furthermore, detail of the detail transmits the field of PSC.
- See the diagram below.

DIAGRAM

Add Natural Person			Add Legal Entity		

S/N	NAME	TELEPHONE	EMAIL	CONTACT ADDRESS	ACTION

Add Natural Person			Add Legal Entity		

A. NATURAL PERSON DETAILS

Tax Residency

Tax Identification Number

Surname	First Name	Other Name

Date of Birth

Gender

Nationality

Contact Details

Phone number +234	Email	Occupation

Address

The address of the PSC

Country	State	LGA

Post Code	City/Town/Village	House Number/Building Name

Street Name

- Use Service Address as Residential Address

RESIDENTIAL ADDRESS

The home address of the PSC (not for publication) Individual's residential address. You can state 'Same as service address' in this section if the usual residential address is the same as the service address.

You cannot state 'Same as service address' if the service address has stated as the Company's Registered Office'. You will need to complete the address in full. This address cannot be a P O Box number.

Country	State	LGA

City/Town/Village	Post Code	House Number/Building Name

Street Name

Means of Identification

Type

	Identity Number

B. Details of PSC Affiliation
- Does the PSC above have any affiliation?

C. Details of Politically Exposed Person (PEP)

A Politically Exposed Person (PEP) is a person who has been entrusted with a prominent public position and their family members and close associates.

- Is the individual named above a PEP?

Interests held.

Shares in a company or interest in a limited liability partnership

Details of the interest (s) held

Does the PSC directly hold at least 5% of the shares or interest in a company or limited liability partnership?   Yes   **No**

Does the PSC indirectly hold at least 5% of the shares or interest in a company or limited liability partnership?   Yes   **No**

Does the PSC directly hold at least 5% of the voting rights in a company or limited liability partnership?   Yes   **No**

Does the PSC indirectly hold at least 5% of the voting rights in a company or limited liability partnership?   Yes   **No**

The right to appoint or remove a majority of the directors or partners

Does the PSC hold the right to appoint or remove a majority of the directors or partners in a company or limited liability partnership   Yes   **No**

Significant influence or control over a company or limited partnership

Does the PSC otherwise have the right to exercise or is exercising significant influence or control over a company or limited liability partnership?   Yes   **No**

Significant influence or control whether or not the PSC is a legal entity, but would itself satisfy any of the first four conditions if it were an individual? Yes **No**

Add PSC

A PERSON WITH SIGNIFICANT CONTROL

S/N	Name	Telephone	Email	Contact Address	Action
1	Peace Abah	07012345678	Peaceabah123@gmail.com	101/A, Fine villa Maitama, Amac, FCT, Nigeria	Edit Delete

Back   **Save & Continue**

Step 2. (h).   **Statement of Compliance**.

- Please complete this section if this application is delivered by an applicant or an accredited agent.

NOTE: If this application is delivered by an applicant or an accredited agent other than a legal practitioner. If you are a legal practitioner, the statement of compliance can be made by one of the first directors/subscribers or upload a separate declaration of compliance.

Step 2 (i).   **Document Upload.**

Documents required to be uploaded include mandatory and optional documents; the mandatory document includes:

- The means of identification of the directors, shareholders, and witnesses are to be compiled into one pdf document. In case of corporate director/secretary or shareholder the certificate for the said certificate should be attached herein.
- The signatures of every director and shareholder in jpeg/image separately.
- The signature of every PSC (JPEG or PNG image) separately
- Signature of the Deponent (Accredited agent signature) in Jpeg or PNG image.
- Signature of the witness in JPEG or PNG image.
- Optional documents include a certificate of incorporation for foreign corporate shareholders translated if not in English (where applicable).
- Reason for restriction of residential address of the director/shareholder/PSC/Deponent or witness. Note that, the restricted residential address of any of the above attracts a charge of N25,000.00.
- Statutory declaration of compliance for legal practitioners.
- On the part of other documents in pdf (upload the secretary's signature under this option) etc.
- Ensure the documents uploaded fit the actions and needs. Save and continue.

See diagram on the below.

S/N	Document	File format	Is required	Upload	STATUS	ACTION
1	Means Of Identification	Pdf	Yes	Upload		
2	Signature Of Joy Peters (Witness)	Jpeg/Png Image	Yes	Upload		
3	Signature Of Peace Abah (Director)	Jpeg/Png	Yes	Upload		
4	Signature Of Peace Abah (Shareholder)	Jpeg/Png	Yes	Upload		
5	Signature Of Peace Abah (Psc)	Jpeg/Png	Yes	Upload		
6	Signature Of (The Deponent)	Jpeg/Png Image	Yes	Upload		
7	Certificate Of Incorporation For Foreign Corporate Shareholder - Translated If Not In English (Where Applicable)	Pdf	Optional	Upload		
8	Reason For	Pdf	Optional	Upload		

	Restriction of Residential Address of Joy Peters (Witness)				

9	Reason For Restriction Of Residential Address Of Peace Abah (Director)	Pdf	Optional	Upload	
10	Reason For Restriction Of Residential Address Of Peace Abah Shareholder)	Pdf	Optional	Upload	
11	Reason For Restriction Of Residential Address Of Peace Abah (Psc)	Pdf	Optional	Upload	
12	Reason For Restriction Of Residential Address Of The Deponent	Pdf	Optional	Upload	
13	Statutory Declaration Of Compliance For	Pdf	Optional	Upload	

	Legal Practitioners					
14	Others	Pdf	Optional	Upload		

Back   **Save & Continue**

Step 2(j).   **Preview**

- This entails a checklist of your work from A -I.

Step 2(k).   **Payment of Registration fee and Stamp Duty.**

- See the previous payment procedure.
- Unlike payment for creating an account, two payments would be made for company registration, and they are split into registration fee and stamp duty fee.
- Ensure you have a suitable network while carrying out both payments.
- Upon successful payment, the work would be transmitted from not submitted to pending approval.
- A clear and detailed work need not be queried.
- Upon approval, download the three documents (The certificate of registration, status report, and memorandum of association) on or before the 7 days of grace (7 days including the day it was approved).

Content of a complete Certificate.

1. A complete company certificate shall have the registered name, RC number, Nigerian Coat of Arms, seal of the corporate Affairs Commission, signature of the Registrar general on the face of the certificate.

2. A complete company certificate must have the 12-digit Tax Identification Number on the face of the certificate. Where the certificate happens to have no TIN, report it to CAC by sending mail to SPU@cac.gov.ng with the subject update status, stating the omission on the certificate, the company, and the RC number, OR send a complaint to the Support Center through the post-incorporation portal.

NOTE: Any issue of omission on the content of the certificate should be reported within seven days of approval, as the issue will be treated without a charge.

Note: Any other issue with the downloaded documents should be reported within seven days of grace. Issues such as:

a. Head address of the company not stated in the status report.
b. Switching the genders of the directors, shareholders, etc. These will be resolved without a fine.

Having completed registration for a private company, other registrations follow similar pattern.

HOW TO AVOID/ANSWER QUERY.

1. Be certain in the choice of name you choose. The business name should not take the form and wording of an incorporated trustee. The company's name should not contain restricted or prohibited words.
2. Acronyms used in name reservations should be supported with the acronym's meaning.
3. Clarity in the nature and description of the business. A general contract should be defined.
4. Unknown street address should be stated along with the name of the State.

5. Uploading the ID CARD; where there is more than one proprietor, director, or trustee, the ID cards should be compiled in one PDF format and uploaded in the means of identification box.

6. The means of identification must be valid; check the expiration date of the driver's license, the national identity card, and any others.

7. Issues of share capital should be treated with clear arithmetic; the issued share capital must fully be taken up. Also, the division of share capital should be divided by the total shares, unless otherwise stated.

8. Avoid duplication; issues of duplicate directors, shareholders, secretaries, or PSCs should be dictated and treated before uploading their signatures.

9. The registration of a company that involves monetary transactions or securities investment (banking) should comply with the share capital percent stated for it.

10. Every other query should be treated literally, as stated.

3.2   POST INCORPORATION

This comprises every activity, changes, amendment, and filing done after the becoming of a legal entity. This also includes; Alteration of memorandum, annual returns filing, Appointments of Administrator, Receiver, Receiver Manager, or supervisor, Certified true copy/Certified Extracts, Change of Company Secretary, Change of Director, Change in Trustee, Change in allotment of shares, change of name, Change of registered address, company search, Conversion/Re-Registration of company, Notice/change of person with significant control, Notice of cessation to act as a receiver, manager, Administrator, or Supervisor, increase in issued share capital, notice of change in particulars of director, notice of change in particulars of shareholder, Reduction in issued share capital. Registration of Charges, Statement of Satisfaction in whole or in part of a charge, Transmission| Transfer| Surrender| New Allotment, liquidation/winding up and request for letter of good standing. Other post-incorporation activities that are important to the operation of every company include compliance with regulatory bodies related to their lines of business, Intellectual property protection, risk management, etc.

For practice, this chapter detailed more on annual return and its filing for business name and company.

3.2.1   **ANNUAL RETURN**

An annual return is the return that an investment provides over a period, expressed as a time-weighted annual percentage.

It is a statutory requirement that every business, company, or incorporated trustee in Nigeria must fulfill its yearly obligation, which keeps the commission aware that the company is in line with its business activities.

> Every company shall, once at least every year, make and deliver to the Commission an annual return in the form specified under sections **418, 419, or 420** as may be applicable.
>
> Provided that a company need not make a return under this section either in the year of its incorporation or, if it is not required by Section 237 to hold an annual general meeting during the following year, in that year.[22]

Company Liable to File Annual Returns.

Every incorporated entity is expected to file its annual return on the due date as specified in its status report.

These include business names, private companies, public companies, limited partnerships, company limited by guarantee and incorporated trustees.

Requirement, Calculation, and Due Date of Filing Annual Return Under CAMA

Business name (sole proprietor, partnership, enterprise, ventures, etc.)

The prescribed duration for any business annual return is 18 months from the date of its incorporation and subsequently every year after the first annual return date.

---

[22] Companies and Allied matters Act. Cap. C 20 Laws of the Federation of Nigeria 2020, Section 417.

- The annual return for the business name should be filed no later than June 30th of every year. However, businesses whose months of return are not June are still in line to file upon their due date.

<u>Company.</u>

The annual return of a company shall be at the eighteen months of its incorporation. In other words, a year and six months of its incorporation and a yearly interval thereafter.

Section 418 (1). The annual return by a company having shares other than a small company shall contain the registered office of the company, registers of members and debenture holders, shares and debentures, indebtedness, past and present members, directors, and secretary.[23] It shall also accompany the financial/audited statement of account for the year in view. On the other hand, annual return for a small company shall contain the information set out in **Section 418 (1)** above, and a financial statement of account as an optional document.

3.2.2   Annual Return for a Business Name.

Step 1. Enter in your Browser post.cac.gov.ng/login.

Login

Log in to your portal.

Username
Password
Forgot password? Click here
Login

---

[23] Ibid., Section 418.

Enter your username and password before clicking on login.

Step 2. Enter the business name or Business registration number and click on search.

- Click on Proceed to Dashboard upon display of the company details. See below.

Dashboard	Search	Search	Username	Logout

Post-incorporation Services

Accredited Agent Dashboard

Company search

3653594

Search

Search Result

S/N	Company Name	Registration number	Entity Types	address	Date of registration	Action
1	CEA & Partners	3653594	Business name	Abuja	1/1/2021	**Proceed to Dashboard**

Step 3.

Click on Annual return to commence your filing.

Business Name
Annual Return

CEA AND PARTNERS	0 Not Submitted	0 Pending Approval	0 Queried	0 Approved

Start Annual Returns

Annual Returns
Cessation
Change of name
Change of nature of business
Change of proprietor/partner (s).
Change of principal place of Business address and/or branch address.
Edit proprietor/partner(s) information.
Certified True Copy/certified Extracts
Business name status report
Request Letter of Good Standing.

Step 4. Click on Start Annual Return process as displayed.

Step 5. Annual Returns-Form

- The first annual return must be made after 18 months of business incorporation. Subsequent ones are to be calculated yearly.

Fill in the annual return form.

a. The principal business activity classifications (1) and (2).

b. The principal activity description

c. The principal place of the business

d. Branch address to the business if the same was provided during incorporation.

e. Particulars of the Proprietor or Partners of the business (Name and details of the proprietor; the date of birth, phone number, occupation, email, State, city, LGA, house number, and street. address and means of identification)

f. Specify the type of proprietor or partner (s). and Click on Add.

g. Annual Return Details: (the annual return year, the financial year start, and the financial year end). Example: April 1 to April 1st of the following year.

h. The turnover and net assets. To calculate turnover, divide the number of new securities purchased and the number of securities sold by the total assets under management. Net assets are the value of a company's assets minus its liabilities.

i. Authentication. By typing the name of the proprietor or any of the partners of the business, or any authorized person.

See the diagram below.

Annual Returns Dashboard/Requirement/Annual Returns Form

1. Annual Returns	2. Preview	3. Payment	4. uploads

Business Name Details.

Business name	Registration Number
DICE ENTERPRISE	3653594

General Nature of Business.

Principal Business Activity Classification 1.   Principal Business Activity Classification 2.

Other Service activities	Film production services.

Principal Activity Description

To carry on the business of film production, music production, and other artistic display

Principal Place of Business.

State

	LGA	City/Town/Village
FCT	AMAC	Abuja

Postcode   House Number/Building Name

	NO. 1

Street

Empress Plaza, Wuse.

Branch Address (if any)

Branch State

	Branch LGA	Branch City

Branch House Number/Building Name   Branch Postal Code

Branch Street Name

Particulars of Proprietor/ Partners

Proprietor/Partner (s) type

Individual Proprietor

Personal Details

Surname	First Name	Other Name
Abah	Peace	

Date of Birth	Gender	Nationality
01/04/1996	Female	Nigeria

Former Name (If any)	Former Nationality (If any)

Contact Details

Phone Number	Email	Occupation
07012345678	abahpeace123@gmail.com	Lawyer

Service Address

State	LGA
FCT	AMAC

Post Code	City/Town/Village	House NO/Building Name
	Abuja	NO. 1

Street Name
Empress Plaza, Wuse, Abuja.

Residential Address

Country	State	LGA
Nigeria	FCT	AMAC

City/Town/Village	Post Code	House NO/Building Name
Abuja		NO. 1

Means of Identification

Types

NIN	12345678901

※**Add partners**※

Proprietor/Partner(s)

S/N	NAME	TELEPHONE	EMAIL	TYPE	ACTION
1	Abah Peace	07012345678	abahpeace@gmail.com	Individual proprietor	Edit delete

New company within the last 18 months – can't file annual returns yet

Annual Returns Details

Annual Return for the year financial year start financial year end/accounting year end.

2022	07/01/2022	07/01/2023

TURN OVER(NAIRA)   NET ASSETS (NAIRA)

N100,000.00	N50,000.00

Authentication

This form is authorized by a proprietor, partner, or any authorized person.

Name   Description

Abah Peace	proprietor.

Back   **save & continue.**

Steps 6-7 and 8

- Preview (checkmate the work done on step 5)

- Payment. (Prescribed fee of N3000.00 for those within the time or N8000.00 for defaults) See the previous payment page for payment procedures.
- Upload. Upon upload, the work is transferred to the second column that is pending approval.
- Work can either be queried if not duly filed or approved if it is in line with the procedure.
- Download the approved acknowledgement letter.

4.3   **Annual Returns for a Company.**

Required documents to be annexed for a private company.

1. A certificate signed by both the director and the secretary of the company that the company has not, since it's the date of its last return or, in the case of a first return, since the date of the incorporation of the company issued any invitation to the public to subscribe for shares or debentures of the company, issued any invitation to the public to subscribe for shares or debentures of the company... See **Section 423**[24]

2. Certificate specifying the type of company if it is a small company. (1 and 2 are not mandatory requirements)

3. The amount of its turnover for that year is not more than N120,000,000 or such amount as may be fixed by the commission.

4. Its net asset value is not more than N60,000,000 or such amount as may fixed by the commission.

5. None of its members is an alien.

6. None of its members is a government official, a government agent, or a nominee.

---

[24] Companies and Allied matters Act. Cap. C 20 Laws of the Federation of Nigeria 2020,Section 423 (1).

7. The directors among them hold at least 51% of the equity share capital of the company.[25]

8. Provision of financial statements (statement of cash flow) of the company. Thus, a modified financial statement or balance sheet shall state:

   - The name of the company, the period it covered, a brief description of its activities, and its legal forms.[26]
   - A copy of the modified balance sheet shall be signed as required by **Section 386** of this Act.
   - The company's balance sheet shall contain a statement by the directors that they rely on **sections 393 to 397** of this Act as entitling them to deliver modified accounts and do so on the ground that the company and the statement shall appear in the balance sheet immediately above the signatures of the directors.[27]

   Note: The financial statement needs to be prepared by an auditor.

Note: Annual return filing cannot be an avenue to cure the needs of the directors, shareholders, or PSC default. Thus, adding or removing any of the above bodies would not be reflected in the company documents.

<u>Penalty for non-compliance with the annual return</u>.

- Failure to file an annual return for a consecutive period of 10 years is a good ground for striking the name of a company off the company's registrar.[28]

---

[25] Companies and Allied matters Act. Cap. C 20 Laws of the Federation of Nigeria 2020,Section 423 (2) ()1 (a-f).

[26] First Schedule of the Companies and Allied matters Act. Cap. C 20 Laws of the Federation of Nigeria 2020.

[27] Sixth Schedule of Companies and Allied Matter Act. 2020.

[28] Ibid., Section 425(3).

3.2.3 Pictorial Filing of Annual Return for a private company limited by shares. (Small Company)

Step 1. Follow the steps above, log in to your accredited portal.

Step 2. Fill in the company name or RC number on the dashboard and click on search. Followed by proceeding with the dashboard.

Accredited Agent Dashboard.
Company Search

1234567

Search

Search Result

S/N	Company Name	Registration Number	Entity Types	address	Date of registration	Action
1	CEA NIG LTD	1234567	Company	Abuja	1/1/2021	Proceed to Dashboard

Step 3. Click on the annual return and start filing.

Post-Incorporation Services Have
a Complaint?

Company.

Company

Annual Returns

CEA Nig LTD Reg Number. 1234567	0 Not submitted	0 Pending Approval	0 Queried	0 approved

START ANNUAL RETURN

Alteration of memorandum
Annual Returns
Appointments of Administrator, Receiver, Receiver Manager, or supervisor.
Certified true copy/ Certified Extracts
Change of Company Secretary
Change of Director.
Change in allotment of shares
Change of Name
Change of Registered Address
Company search
Conversion/ReRegistration of company
Notice/change of person with significant control
Notice of cessation to act as a receiver, manager, Administrator, or Supervisor

Increase in issued Share Capital
Notice of change in Particulars of Director
Notice of change in Particulars of Shareholders
Reduction in issued share capital.
Registration of Charges.
Statement of Satisfaction in whole or in part of a charge.
Transmission| Transfer| Surrender| New Allotment
Liquidation/winding up
Request for letter of Good standing
Fourteenth Schedule

Step 4. Requirements.

1. Duly completed annual return form
2. Please fill out the form below.
3. Click on proceed.

Registered name	Registration number	Classification	
CEA Nigeria LTD	1234567	Company	**Proceed**

Step 5. The annual return form.

Home/Dashboard/ CEA NIG LTD/ Data Entry

1. Annual Returns	2. PSC Details	3. Preview	4. Payment

Company Details.

Company Name in Full | Company RC Number

CEA NIG LTD	1234567

Annual Return made up to the   Day of   Year

Enter the day	Enter the month	

(Being the fourteen days after

The day of the general meeting

For the year)

Date of the general meeting. The
annual return must be delivered,
within 14 days of the date given
Below.

Please show the business classification code number (s) for the principal entity or activities

Classification code 1.   Classification code 2.

If you cannot determine the code, please give a brief description of your business activity below:

Principal Activity Description

Please confirm your company type by ticking the appropriate box below (only one box must be ticked)

- Small Company
  Private company limited by shares (other than small) Company limited by guarantee.
  Public Company

Registered office address

Number/building name   Street name

City   State

LGA

Head office location if different from office registered address.

Number/building name   Street name

City   State

LGA

Location of Register of members/Register of a person with significant control (if applicable)

Number/Building name   street name

<table>
<tr><td></td><td></td></tr>
</table>

City   State

<table>
<tr><td></td><td></td></tr>
</table>

LGA

<table>
<tr><td></td></tr>
</table>

Officers of the company.

New Appointments

You cannot use this form to appoint new officers to the company. To do this please complete the appropriate form and submit it together with this annual return form.

Change of officer details

You cannot use this form to change any officers 'details. To do this please complete the appropriate form and submit it together with this annual return form.

Corporate secretary's details

Add corporate secretary

Individual secretary's details

Add individual secretary

Current secretary' details

Director's details

Add director

Current director's details
Emeka Okoye
Emeka123@gmail.com | 07012345678
Yakubu Mohad
Yakubum123@gmail.com| 08012345678
 Oluwa Adeyemi
Adeyemi311@gmail.com | 09012345678
Statement of issued share capital.

Class of shares (ordinary share)	Number of shares | inputted value: 1,000,000
Ordinary	1000000

Aggregate nominal value	Total aggregate amount unpaid if any
N 1000000.00	N

Class of shares (Preference share)	Number of shares | inputted value:
Preference	

Aggregate nominal value	Total aggregate amount paid if any.

Total

Number of shares	Total aggregate nominal value	Total aggregate amount unpaid

Statement of capital (Prescribed particulars of right attached to the shares)

Class of shares

Prescribed particulars of the right attached to shares.

The particulars are:

1. Particulars of voting rights, including rights that arise only in certain circumstances.

2. Particulars of any right, concerning dividends, to participate in a distribution.

3. Particulars of any right concerning capital, to participate in a distribution (including winding up) and

4. Whether the shares are to be redeemed or are liable to be redeemed at the option of the company or the shareholder and any terms or conditions relating to redemption of these shares.

Particulars of indebtedness

Total amount of indebtedness of the company in respect of all mortgagees which are required to be registered with the commission under the Companies and Allied Matters Act (CAMA)

N

Particulars of Turnover and Net Assets (this applies to small companies that are not required to submit financial statements)

Total Turnover for the year (Naira)	Total Turnover for the year (Amount in words)

Total value of Net Assets for the year (Naira)	Total value of Net Assets for the year (in words)

List of past and present members.

Members are the shareholders of a company.

List of persons holding shares or stock in the company on the fourteenth day of the annual general meeting for

Enter the year. Eg 2022

And of a person who held shares or stock therein at any time since the date of the return, or, in the cases of the first return of the incorporation of the company.

Add individual member	Add corporate member

Emeka Okoye

Emeka123@gmail.com | 07012345678

500000 ordinary shares

Yakubu Mohad

Yakubum123@gmail.com| 08012345678

250000 ordinary shares

Oluwa Adeyemi

Adeyemi311@gmail.com | 09012345678

250000 ordinary shares

Authentication

This form is authorized by a Director, Secretary, or any authorized officer of the company.

Full name (s)

Description

Diagram of filled form

1. Annual Returns 3	2. PSC Details	3. Preview	4. Payment

Company Details.

Company Name in Full	Company RC Number
CEA NIG LTD	1234567

Annual Return made up to the	Day of	Year
1st	07	2022

(Being the fourteen days after

The day of the general meeting

For the year)

Date of the general meeting

The annual return must be delivered,

within 14 days of the date given Below.

18/06/2023

Please show the business classification code number (s) for the principal entity or activities

Classification code 1.   Classification code 2.

Other personal services	Other personal services

If you cannot determine the code, please give a brief description of your business activity below:

Principal Activity Description

Legal practice

Please confirm your company type by ticking the appropriate box below (only one box must be ticked)

- Small Company

  Private company limited by shares (other than small)
  Company limited by guarantee.

  Public Company

Registered office address

Number/building name   Street name

101/A	Fine villa Maitama

City   State

Abuja	FCT

LGA

AMAC

Head office location if different from office registered address.

Number/building name   Street name

City

State

LGA

Location of Register of members/Register of a person with significant control (if applicable)

Number/Building name   street name

City   State

LGA

Officers of the company.

New Appointments

You cannot use this form to appoint new officers to the company. To do this please complete the appropriate form and submit it together with this annual return form. Change of officer details You cannot use this form to change any officers' details. To do this please complete the appropriate form and submit it together with this annual return form.

Corporate secretary's details

Add corporate secretary

Individual secretary's details

Add individual secretary

Current secretary' details

Director's details

Add director

Current director's details

Emeka Okoye

Emeka123@gmail.com | 07012345678

YakubuMohad

Yakubum123@gmail.com| 08012345678

Oluwa Adeyemi

Adeyemi311@gmail.com | 09012345678

Statement of issued share capital

Class of shares (ordinary share)	Number of shares | inputted value: 1,000,000
Ordinary	1000000

Aggregate nominal value	Total aggregate amount unpaid, if any
N. 1000000.00	N

Class of Shares (Preference share)	Number of Shares| inputted value:
Preference	

Aggregate nominal value	Total aggregate amount paid if any

Total

Number of shares	Total aggregate nominal value	Total aggregate amount unpaid

Statement of capital (Prescribed particulars of right attached to the shares)

Class of shares

EQUITY (ORDINARY) SHARES

Prescribed particulars of right attached to shares. The particulars are:

- Particulars of voting rights, including rights that arise only in certain circumstances.
- Particulars of any right, concerning dividends, to participate in a distribution.
- Particulars of any right concerning capital, to participate in a distribution (including winding up) and
- Whether the shares are to be redeemed or are liable to be redeemed at the option of the company or the shareholder and any terms or conditions relating to redemption of these shares.

Particulars of indebtedness

Total amount of indebtedness of the company in respect of all mortgagees which are required to be registered with the commission under the Companies and Allied Matters Act (CAMA)

N

Particulars of Turnover and Net Assets (this applies to small companies that are not required to submit financial statements)

Total Turnover for the year (Naira)	Total Turnover for the year (Amount in words)
#120,000.00	One Hundred and Twenty Thousand naira

Total value of Net Assets for the year (Naira)	Total value of Net Assets for the year (in words)
#60,000	Sixty Thousand naira

List of past and present members.

Members are the shareholders of a company.

List of persons holding shares or stock in the company on the fourteenth day of the annual general meeting for

Enter the year. (Enter the current year you are filing).

And of a person who held shares or stock therein at any time since the date of the return, or, in the cases of the first return of the incorporation of the company.

Add individual member	Add corporate member

Emeka Okoye
Emeka123@gmail.com | 07012345678
500000 ordinary shares
Yakubu Mohad
Yakubum123@gmSail.com| 08012345678
250000 ordinary shares
Oluwa Adeyemi

Adeyemi311@gmail.com | 09012345678

250000 ordinary shares

Authentication

This form is authorized by a Director, Secretary, or any authorized officer of the company.

Fullname (s)

EMEKA OKOYE

Description

DIRECTOR

BACK   **SAVE & CONTINUE**

STEP 6.   PERSON OF SIGNIFICANT CONTROL

1. Annual Return Details	**2. PSC DETAILS**	3. PREVIEW	4. PAYMENT

Company Details

Company name in full.   Company RC number

CEA NIG LTD	123456

A person with Significant Control details

PSCs are shareholders with a threshold of at least 5% of the shares of a company.

Emeka Okoye

Emeka123@gmail.com | 07012345678   Delete   Edit

Yakubu Mohad
Yakubum123@gmail.com| 08012345678   Delete   Edit

Oluwa Adeyemi
Adeyemi311@gmail.com | 09012345678   Delete   Edit.

Add PSC

Back   **Save & Continue**

STEP 7 and 8.   PREVIEW and PAYMENT.

Peruse your work and make the payment using any of the convenient options.

After successful payment click on the upload document and submit the Application

Documents must be in Portable Document formats (PDF) only.

Document	Status
Others	

Submit Application.

Tips to Note//

- On filling the form of Annual Return for companies with undisplayed details such as lack of director, secretary, shareholder, or PSC. Obtain the information needed and add the missing ones. (The above is to comply with the due filing of the annual return form without query).

- Financial statements: this is optional for small companies as it would not restrict submission nor approval of the work.
- The issue of no PSC can lead to a query, add a PSC using the shareholder's information.
- The addition of a director or PSC does not transmit to change in the company information as such will not reflect in the company's status report.
- Query: could be on grounds of undue date for annual return, check the expected date (18 months) for first annual return and 12 months for subsequent years and comply with same or form.
- Penalty: N5000 for any company in default.
- Acknowledgement letter: to be downloaded once the work is approved.

Chapter 4.

4.1   **INCORPORATED TRUSTEE.**

This comprises a group of two or more bodies that are appointed by any community of persons bound together by custom, religion, kinship, or nationality or by anybody or association of persons established for religious, educational, literary, scientific, social, development, cultural, sporting or charitable purpose, they may if so authorized by the community, body or association apply to the commission in the manner provided for registration under this Act as a corporate body.[29] See **Section 823** of the Companies and Allied Matters Act as amended.

CATEGORIES OF AN INCORPORATED TRUSTEE.

This could be

1. Faith Based Association such as churches, mosques, etc
2. Social Clubs Based Associations such as peer clubs, agemates, and other social gatherings.
3. Cultural Based Association
4. Sporting Based Association
5. Foundation Based Association and
6. Community-Based Association.

4.1.1   **QUALIFICATION OF A TRUSTEE[30]**

Section 826 of the Act provides that a person shall not be qualified to be appointed or act as a trustee if-

     a. He is an infant.

     b. He is a person of unsound mind having been so found guilty by a court.

     c. He is an undischarged bankrupt or

     d. He has been convicted of an offence involving fraud or dishonesty within five years of his proposed appointment.

---

[29] Section 823. CAMA 2020 as amended.
[30] Section 826. CAMA 2020 as Amended.

The above constitutes the declaration form's content.

4.1.2   REQUIREMENT FOR AN INCORPORATED TRUSTEE[31].

- Three proposed names[32]
- Email of the association, registered office address, state, LGA, city, house number, and street name.
- Constitution of the Association which can now be filled online. The constitution shall state the name of the association, the aims and objectives of the association, the tenure, power, and duties of the trustees, the governing body, the custody of the common seal, and the meeting of the association. **See also Section 827 of the Act.**[33]
- Aims and Objectives of the organization which shall be for the advancement of any religious, educational, literacy, scientific, social, development, cultural, sporting, or charitable purpose and shall be lawful.[34]
- Name of the trustees; the chairman, secretary, and other trustees. Their addresses, date of birth, occupation, phone number, email address, Nationality, state, LGA, city, house number, street name, and identification card.
- Duly signed minutes of the meeting of the association, appointing the trustees and the number of people present and the vote cast. The minutes shall also contain the special clause.
- Declaration form of the trustee which must be notarized or commissioned by a notary public or commissioner of oath respectively.
- Identification cards of all the trustees.
- Publication in two national daily newspapers which are subjected to the satisfaction of the commission and public objection. Any objection emanating from the advertisement shall be forwarded to the commission within 28 days of the last date of the publication in the newspaper. [35]

---

[31] Section 825 (1) and (2). CAMA 2020 as amended.
[32] Section 825 (1a)
[33] Cap C20
[34] Section 825 (b) CAMA 2020as amended.
[35] Section 828 (1) & (2)

4.1.3 RESERVATION AND APPLICATION OF CONSENT FOR INCORPORATED TRUSTEE.

Name reservation/Application of Consent.

Log in to our portal and click on new Name Reservation

0 NOT SUBMITTED	0 PENDING/QUERIED	0 DENIED	0 RESERVED

※ **New Name Reservation.**

Registration

NOT SUBMITTED	PENDING APPROVAL	QUERIED	APPROVED

STEP 1

1. Name and Type	2. Objectives	3. Preview	4. Payment

Company Type

Classification.	Specific Type
Incorporated Trustee	Incorporated Trustee

Proposed Names

Option 1.	Option 2
Great church of God	Great Church of God

Option 3	Reason for Availability Search
Great Church of God	Change of name
	Name substitution
	New incorporation/Registration

Restricted words, incorporated trustees, and companies limited by guarantee require reservation codes, Any Group Holdings/Consortium also requires reservation codes.

Fill the form above and click on

Apply for Reservation Code

Back   Save & Continue

Step 2.

Incorporated Trustee Details	Constitution	Aims & Objective	Trustee	Document upload	Preview	payment

Incorporated Trustee of Great Church of God

Classification of the Association Class. 1   Classification of the Association Class. 2

Faith-Based Association	Church

Description of the Association's Classification

Propagation of the word of God and services to humanity.

Email

greatchurchgod@gmail.com

Registered Office Address

State	LGA	City/Town/Village
FCT	AMAC	Abuja

Postcode	House number/Building Name
	101/A

street

Fine Villa Maitama, Abuja

Back   **Save &Continue**

Step 3. Constitution

Incorporated Trustee Details	**Constitution**	Aims & Objective	Trustee	Document upload	Preview	payment

Incorporated Trustee of Great Church of God.

Minimum Number of Trustees	Maximum Number of Trustees
2	10

Trustee Tenure

Five

Custody of common seal

secretary

Governing body

Application of funds

Keeping account

Back   **Save & Continue**

Template for Governing Body

The governing body of the association shall be the chairman 2. Vice chairman 3. General secretary 4. Assistant general secretary 5. Financial secretary 6. Treasurer 7. Public relations officer (pro) 8. Provosts 9. Patron's duties/functions of the governing body: A. Chairman. The chairman presides and directs all the affairs, operations, and proceedings of the meetings in accordance with the provisions of the constitution. ii. He shall direct the affairs of the association in accordance with the constitution. iii. He must be a signatory of the association's bank account. iv. Shall be an active member and has the casting vote in a case of tie at a meeting. v. He directs and instructs other officers under him vi. He shall be the association 's chief executive and chairman of the executive committee. B. Vice-chairman: i. Assists the chairman. ii. Performs the functions of the president during meetings and any other gatherings in the absence of the chairman. iii. Takes over the leadership where a vacuum is created by the absence or otherwise of the chairman until a bye-election is effected. C. General secretary i. Maintains the records of proceedings at meetings. ii. Deals with all correspondence of the association. iii. Prepares annual reports of activities. iv. Keeps custody of books, records, and up-to-date nominal roll of members. v. Draws up the agenda of meetings. vi. Issues circulars of meeting or information vii. He summons meetings in emergencies in consultation with the president or the vice chairman, where the chairman is not available viii. She/he must be a signatory to the initiative's bank account. D. Assistant general secretary: i. Assists the secretary ii. Deputies in the absence of the secretary. E. Financial secretary: i. Responsible for the collection and recording of financial or monetary transactions. ii. Keeps proper financial records. iii. Render all monies received to the treasurer for safekeeping and banking. iv. Prepares financial report/statement of income and expenditure. v. He/she must be a signatory to the foundation's bank account. F. Treasurer: i. He receives all monies accruing to the association of custody. ii. He must lodge all monies received in the bank account of the association within 48 hours iii. He is to make the foundation's fund available when requested to do so. Such request must be by the approval of the association which will be signed by the chairman and financial secretary. iv. He shall issue receipts where and when necessary v. He/she must be a signatory to the association's bank account. Public relations officer (pro) i. He acts as the public relations officer of the association. ii. Disseminates information concerning the association within and outside the initiative provosts i. He ensures the maintenance of law and order during meetings and gatherings ii. He ensures orderliness in speaking and good behavior iii. Effects disciplinary measures when necessary during meetings and gatherings. The patrons are regarded as the fathers of this foundation. Their duties are to maintain peace and unity and to see for the smooth and effective administration in the events of facts. They are to give useful information and advice.

Template for application of funds.

The funds shall be applied to achieving the aims and objectives of the foundation. The disbursement of the association funds shall be approved by the Chairman.

Template for keeping account.

The association shall operate a bank account in its name. The signatories to the account shall be the chairman, the financial secretary, and the treasurer. All monies must be paid into the account immediately upon receipt and on no account shall the treasurer keep a cash of more than #10,000.00 with him/her at any point in time. Finance year the shall be from 1st January to 31st of December.

Step 4. Aims and Objective

Incorporated Trustee of Great Church of God

Please note that you must enter at least one object to proceed.

Add Aims/Objectives

Back   **Save & Continue**

Add Aims/Objectives

To preach the word of God	Edit Delete
To assist the less privileged	Edit Delete
To collaborate with other non-for-profit associations	Edit Delete

Back   **Save & Continue**

Step 5. **Trustee**

Incorporated Trustee Details	Constitution	Aims & Objective	**Trustee**	Document upload	Preview	payment

Please note that you must have Two (2) Trustees or more to proceed.

Ensure you add both TRUSTEE(S) / SECRETARY. Use the checkbox below to indicate when adding SECRETARY!

Add Trustee	**Autofill Form with NIN**

Personal Details

Surname	First Name	Other Name

Date of Birth	Gender	Nationality

Former Name (if any)	Former Nationality (If any)

Contact Details

Phone number	Email	Occupation

Service Address

Country	State	LGA

Post Code	City/Town/Village	House Number/Building Name

street

- Use Service Address as Residential Address

Residential Address

Country	State	LGA

City/Town/Village	Post Code	House NO/Building Name

Street

- **Hide Residential Address From Public Records?**

This service attracts an additional fee of N25,000

- Means of Identification

Type	Identity Number

Appoint as Chairman (tick if the trustee is also the chairman)

Add as Secretary ONLY (Not as a TRUSTEE. Add as the Secretary ONLY)

Add as Both Trustee and Secretary

Add Trustee

TRUSTEE (S)

S/N	Name	Telephone	Email	Contact Address	Trustee Type	Action
1	Peace Abah	07012345678	Peaceabah123@gmail.com	101/A, Fine villa Maitama, Amac, FCT, Nigeria	Trustee Chairman	Edit Delet
2	Obi Emeka	09123456789	obiemeka@gmail.com	05.Emeka street, amac FCT Abuja, Nigeria	Trustee Secretary	Edit Delet
3	Joy Peters	081234567895	joypeters@gmail.com	67. Prince and Princess, AMAC, Abuja Nigeria	Trustee	Edit Delet

Back   **Save & Continue**

Step 6. **Upload Document**

Incorporated Trustee Details	Constitution	Aims & Objective	Trustee	**Document upload**	Preview	payment

Document Requirement for Reservation Code

No specific document is mentioned, all needed documents will be uploaded on the registration field.

Document	File format	Is required	Upload	STATUS	ACTION
Supporting Document 1	Pdf	Optional	Upload		
Supporting Document 2	Pdf	Optional	Upload		
Supporting Document 3	Pdf	Optional	Upload		

Back   **Save & Continue**

Step 7. and the last step for the reservation code is the preview and Payment. Kindly use the format explained on payment procedure.

4.1.4   REGISTRATION OF INCORPORATED TRUSTEE

Stage 1. Click on the reserved section, and on the top of the reserved name click on Start Registration followed with the form displayed below.

Great Church of God

Quorum

Add Meetings

Back   Save & Continue

Update

S/N	Name	Telephone	Email	Contact Address	Trustee Type	Action
1	Peace Abah	07012345678	Peaceabah123@gmail.com	101/A, Fine villa Maitama, Amac, FCT, Nigeria	Trustee Chairman	Hide residential address from public record This service attracts an additional fee of N25,000

2	Obi Emeka	09123456789	obiemeka@gmail.com	05. Emeka Street, amac FCT Abuja, Nigeria	Trustee Secretary	Hide residential address from public record This service attracts an additional fee of N25,000
3	Joy Peters	081234567895	joypeters@gmail.com	67.Prince and Princess, AMAC, Abuja Nigeria	Trustee	Hide residential address from public record This service attracts an additional fee of N25,000

<u>Content of a Quorum</u>

Click on the Quorum box and type this information: In annual general meeting of the association, 2/3rd of the members shall form a quorum. At extra ordinary meeting, half of the members of the board of trustees shall be the quorum. At the emergency meeting, three members of the association shall form a quorum.

Add Meetings

1. Annual General Meeting
2. Extra-ordinary Meeting
3. Executive committee Meeting, etc.

Minutes of Meeting Template.

FIRST ANNUAL GENERAL MEETING OF GREAT CHURCH OF GOD.

NO. 101/A Fine Villa Maitama Amac, Abuja Nigeria.

MINUTES OF THE BOARD OF TRUSTEES OF GREAT CHURCH OF HELD ON 22ND OF MAY 2021.

Peace Abah called the meeting to order at 2pm. Those in Attendance and constituting a quorum include Peace Abah, Obi Emeka, and Joy Peters. Absent: Nil

Opening Prayer: prayed by Joy Peters

AGENDA

1. Incorporation of the Association
2. Voting pattern
3. Appointment of the Chairman and Secretary
4. Appointment of the First Trustee
5. Adoption of Special Clause in the Constitution.
6. Closing prayer.

INCORPORATION OF THE ASSOCIATION: there was a uniform agreement that the association be incorporated and same was given to the legal adviser of the association Barr. ABC to see to its perfection.

VOTING PATTERN: voting shall be by raising of hands.

APPOINTMENT OF CHAIRMAN AND SECRETARY: The member recommended that the Association appoints a person among them to be their chairman. MOTION moved by Obi Emeka. Seconded and passed without dissent. Voting was carried out by raising of hands of 3 members in support. Peace Abah was nominated and elected as CHAIRMAN while Obi Emeka was nominated and elected as SECRETARY.

APPOINTMENT OF THE FIRST TRUSTEE: The chairman Peace Abah recommended that the Association appoint the First Trustee and proposed the adoption of the constitution. Peace Abah moved that Obi Emeka, Joy Peters, and Peace Abah be appointed as the first trustees of the Association. Seconded and passed without dissent. Voting was carried out by raising of hands of 3 members in support. The following persons were nominated and subsequently appointed by unanimous vote as the first Trustees of the Association.

NAMES	NO VOTES FOR	NO VOTES AGAINST	REMARK
PEACE ABAH	3	NIL	APPOINTED
OBI EMEKA	3	NIL	APPOINTED
JOY PETERS	3	NIL	APPOINTED

MOTION FOR ADOPTION OF SPECIAL CLAUSE IN THE CONSTITUTION.
Joy Peters
moved a motion for the adoption of the Special Clause of the Constitution. Seconded and passed without dissent. Voting was done by the raising of hands of 3 members in support.

NAMES	VOTING PATTERN
PEACE ABAH	SUPPORTED
OBI EMEKA	SUPPORTED
JOY PETERS	SUPPORTED

Our Aims and Objectives

1. To preach the word of God
2. To assist the less privileged
3. To collaborate with other not-for-profit associations

MOTION FOR ADJOURNMENT was moved by Obi Emeka and the closing prayer was said by Joy Peters.
signed
CHAIRMAN.   SECRETARY

Note: The minutes of the meeting must be signed before uploading it as accompany document for registration of Incorporated Trustees.

Stage 2. Source of Income

Great Church of God

Add Source of Income

Back   **Save & Continue**

Example of source of income detail:

1. Accept donations (whether cash and/or kind) from individuals, corporate bodies, local and international associations.
2. receive grants or assistance from individuals, trusts, foundations, and other charitable or philanthropic foundations in Nigeria and elsewhere.

Stage 3. Publication:

Fill in the correct date of the publication, Newspaper name, and page number.

Great Church of God

First Publication

Date	Newspaper	Newspaper Page

Second Publication

Date	Newspaper	Newspaper Page

Back   Save & Continue

Note// The newspaper must be a national daily newspaper. The publication must be due for filing. Implication of uploading a publication without compliance to 28 days attract query.

When is the newspaper due to upload? Time begins to count from the date of that publication to 28days thereafter and at such due for filing on the 29th day.

Declaration form Template.

Passport photograph

CORPORATE AFFAIRS COMMISSION

(Established under the Companies and Allied Matter Act, 2020)

CAC/IT/FORM/002

TRUSTEES DECLARATION

I,____, Male, Adult, Christian, Of
____NIGERIA.

Trustee of the **Great Church of God.**

Do solemnly and sincerely declare as follows: -

a. THAT I am not an infant.

b. THAT I am not a person of unsound mind.

c. THAT I have not been convicted of any offense involving fraud or dishonesty within five years of my proposed appointment as a trustee.

d. THAT I am not an undischarged bankrupt.

THAT I make this solemn declaration conscientiously believing same to be true and correct in accordance with the Oaths Act currently in force.

____

DEPONENT

Sworn to at ____________ on the ___ day of_______2023

BEFORE ME

____

NOTARY PUBLIC

Stage 4. Document Upload.

S/N	Document	File format	Is required	Upload	STATUS	ACTION
1	Means of identification	Pdf	Yes	Upload		
2	Signature of Peace Abah Trustee Chairman)	Jpeg/png image	Yes	Upload		
3	Signature of Obi Emeka (Trustee Secretary)	Jpeg/png	Yes	Upload		
4	Newspaper Publication(S)	PDF	Yes	Upload		
5	Minute of Meetings	PDF	Yes	Upload		
6	Statutory Declaration Form	PDF	Yes	Upload		
7	Details of Current or past Affiliation with any Existing Organization/Association	Jpeg/Png Image	Optional	Upload		
8	Others	Pdf	Optional	Upload		

Stage 5 and 6. Preview and Payment. Used the prescribed format as explained in related fields.

4.1.5   ANNUAL RETURN FOR INCORPORATED TRUSTEE

Section 848 (1). The trustee of the association shall not earlier than 30th June or later than 31st December each year (other than the year in which it is incorporated) submit to the Commission a return showing the name of the association, the names, addresses, and occupations of the trustees and members of the council or governing body, particulars of any land held by the corporate body during the year, and of any change which has taken place in the constitution of the association during the preceding.[36]

Section 848 (2) The return referred to in subsection (1) shall be accompanied by the audited statement of accounts of the association's year return.[37] Note.

1. Non-compliance with the above attracts penalties and payment of default fees.

2. Failure to file an annual return deactivates the status of the association.

3. Failure to file annual returns for a consecutive period of 10 years is ground to strike the name of the company off the company's register.[38]

Diagram illustration for filling of Annual Return

Log in to post-incorporation

Enter in your Browser post.cac.gov.ng/login.

Login

Log in to your portal.

Username
Password
Forgot password? Click here
Login

Enter your username and password before clicking on login.

---

[36] Ibid., Section 848. (1)

[37] Ibid., section 848 (2)

[38] Companies and Allied matters Act. Cap. C 20 Laws of the Federation of Nigeria 2020, Section 425.

Step 2. Enter the Incorporated Trustee name or the IT number and click on search.

Dashboard	Search	Search	Username	Logout

Post-incorporation Services

Accredited Agent Dashboard

Step 1. Company search

65433

Search

Search Result

S/N	Company Name	Registration number	Entity Types	address	Date of registration	Action
1	Great Church of God	65433	Incorporated Trustee	101/A Fine Villa Maitama, Abuja Nigeria	1/1/2021	**Proceed to Dashboard**

Step 2. Click on Annual and Start Annual Return

Great Church of God. Reg Number: 65433	0 Not submitted	0 Pending Approval	0 Queried	0 approved

START ANNUAL RETURN

Annual Returns
Appointments of Chairman

Amendment of Constitution
Change of Name
Change of Registered Address
Change of Trustee
Certified True Copy Request
Increase in issued Share Capital
Change of Secretary
Dissolution
Incorporated Trustee Status Report
Edit Trustee Information
Request for letter of Good standing
Bi-Annual Statement of Affairs of Incorporated Trustees

REQUIREMENTS

- This return should be accompanied by an Audited Account of the Association for the year in which the return is made.
- Annual Returns for incorporated trustees should be filed between 30th June and 31st December.
- Please fill out the form on the next page

NOTE:

Companies and Allied Matters Act, 2020 Section 862.

1. Subject to the provisions of subsections (2) and (3), if any person in any return, report, certificate, balance sheet, or other document required by, or for the purpose of any of the

provisions of this Act, willfully makes a statement which is false in any material particular knowing it to be false, he commits an offense and is liable -

a. on conviction to imprisonment for a term of two years; and

b. in the case of a company, to fine as the Court deems fit for every day the default continues.

2. A company that makes a statement in its annual returns which is false in any material particular shall in respect of each year of any such returns be liable to a penalty prescribed in the Commission's regulations if it is a small company or in any other case.

3. Nothing in this section shall affect the provisions of any enactment imposing penalties in respect of perjury in force in Nigeria.

GO BACK   **START PROCESS**

Registered Name	Registered Number	Classification	
Great Church of God	65433	Incorporated Trustee	**Start**

Step 3.

Annual Returns Dashboard/Requirement/Annual Returns Form

1. **Annual Returns**	2. Preview	3. Payment	4. uploads

Incorporated Trustee
Details

Name of Association   Registration Number

Name of Association	Registration Number
Great Church of God	65443

State	LGA	City/Town/Village
FCT	AMAC	ABUJA

Postcode	House NO/Building Name
	101/A

Street

Fine Villa Maitama, Abuja

Trustee's Details

Personal Details

Surname	First name	Other name
Abah	Peace	

Date of Birth	Gender	Nationality
01/04/1996	female	Nigerian

Former name (if any)	Former Nationality (if any)

Contact Details

Phone Number	Email	occupation
07012345678	abahpeace@gmail.com	Lawyer

Service Address

This is only applicable to TRUSTEES that have already restricted their residential addresses from the public record.

Please state 'Same as service address' in this section if your usual residential address is the same as service address.

State   LGA

FCT	AMAC

Post Code   City/Town/Village   House NO/Building Name

	ABUJA	101/A

Street Name

Fine villa Maitama.

Residential Address.

This is only applicable to TRUSTEES that have already restricted their residential addresses from the public record.

Please state 'Same as service address' in this section if your usual residential address is the same as service address. You cannot state 'Same as service address' if your service address has been stated in the Section above as 'The Association's Registered Office'. You will need to complete the address in full.

State   LGA

City/Town/Village   Post Code   house NO/Building Name

Street Name

Means of Identification

Type   Number

National Identification Card	NIN Number

Add Trustee

Name	Telephone	Email	Contact Address	Trustee Type	Action
Peace Abah	07012345678	Peaceabah123@gmail.com	101/A, Fine villa Maitama, Amac, FCT, Nigeria	Trustee	Edit Delete
Obi Emeka	09123456789	obiemeka@gmail.com	05.Emeka street, amac FCT Abuja, Nigeria	Trustee	Edit Delete
Joy Peters	081234567895	joypeters@gmail.com	67. Prince and Princess, AMAC,Abuja Nigeria	Trustee	Edit Delete

Particulars of the Governing Council (Executives)

Surname	First Name	Other Name
Abah	Peace	

Phone number	Email	Occupation
07012345678	peaceabah123@gmail.com	Lawyer

Service Address

State	LGA
FCT	AMAC

Post Code	City/Town/Village	House NO/Building Name
	Abuja	101/A

Street Name

Fine Villa Maitama

Add Executives

Name	Telephone	Email	Contact Address	Trustee Type	Action
Peace Abah	07012345678	Peaceabah123@gmail.com	101/A, Fine villa Maitama, Amac, FCT, Nigeria	Trustee Chairman	Edit Delete
Obi Emeka	09123456789	obiemeka@gmail.com	05.Emeka street, Amac FCT Abuja, Nigeria	Trustee Secretary44	Edit Delete

Years Filed

S/N	YEARS	STATUS

Years Not Filed

S/N	YEARS	STATUS
1	2022	Was not Filed for

Annual Returns Details
Year of Return

2022

Financial Year Start	Financial Year End
2022-01-01	2022-12-31

Gross Assets (Naira)	Net Asset (Naira)
N120,000	N60000

Bankers	Bank and Balance as at Financial Year End
Zenith Bank	N70,000

Source of Income in the Year	Trustee's Benefits During the Year
Support and Donation	N50,000

Authentication

Name	Description
Peace Abah	Chairman

We certify that the information given in this form is correct to the best of our knowledge and has been brought to the attention of all the trustees.

Back   **Save & Continue**

Steps 4 and 5: Preview and Payment respectively

Checkmate the work and make the needed payment.

After payment, you are expected to upload a document thus a Financial/Audited statement of account prepared by an accountant. After uploading the said document click on submit.

Chapter 5.

CONCLUSION

In conclusion, the comprehensive understanding of corporate transactions, incorporation, and its criteria underscores the critical importance of corporate governance. Corporate practice is inexhaustible. This handbook provides knowledge about corporate transactions and different evolutions to companies' Acts. Recourse should be given to the features of the Companies and Allied Matters Act 2020 as Amended which provides a great gap from the earlier Acts. Knowing that this book emphasizes more on the practical steps to incorporation especially pre-incorporation of business name, company, and Incorporated Trustee it also talks about post incorporation and post-incorporation activities using annual returns for business name, company, and incorporated trustee as home illustration.

In Chapter Three, the need for exact information to file during the annual return and sections to leave vacant are of great importance. A company that has no branch address, Secretary, or default in directors cannot use annual returns as a medium to cure the lapses. Data should not be added on columns such as total aggregate amount unpaid, or particulars of indebtedness except provided by the company's director. On the other hand, improvision can be made on the PSC as this is important to duly completion of the annual returns form.

Fundamental to this handbook is to be an assisting aid to young corporate lawyers.

LIST OF CASES

1. Incorporated Trustees of Holy Apostles Church Ayetoro & Ors. v. INCD Trustees Oneness Faith of Christ Ministry, Ayetoro & Ors. (2016) LPELR41368(CA).
2. Bulet INTL (NIG) LTD &Anor v. Olaniyi & Anor (2017) LPELR-424 75 (SC).
3. Salomon v. Salomon (1897) AC.22
4. United Cement Co. LTD V. LIBEND Group LTD &Anor (2016) LPELR42038 (CA).
5. WEMA Bank v. Nigerian National Shipping Line Limited. (1979) FRCLR 133.
6. CBN v. Igwillo (2007) LPELR-385

TABLE OF STATUTES

1. Companies Ordinance 1972.
2. Companies Act. Laws of the Federation of Nigeria, 1968.
3. Companies and Allied Matters Act. Laws of the Federation of Nigeria, 1990.
4. Companies and Allied Matters Act. Laws of the Federation of Nigeria, 2020 as Amended.

LIST OF FORMS

1. CAC 1: Availability Check and Reservation of Names.
2. CAC 1.1: Application for Registration.
3. CAC 1.1: Continuation Page for First Directors.
4. CAC 2.1: Appointment or Change of Company Secretary.
5. CAC 10: Annual Return for a Small Company.
6. CAC/BN/7: Annual Returns for Business Name.
7. CAC FORMS in the accredited agent user portal.
8. CAC: CRP-User guide.

LIST OF ABBREVIATIONS

- AC: Appeal Cases
- Anor: Another
- CA: Court of Appeal.
- CAC: Corporate Affairs Commission
- CAMA: Companies and Allied Matters Act
- CBN: Central Bank of Nigeria
- HMO: Health Maintenance Organization.
- IATA: International Air Travel Agency
- LLP: Limited Liability Partnership
- LPELR: Law Pavilion Electronic Law Report
- LTD: Limited
- N/B: Note Before
- NAICOM: National Insurance Commission
- NASA: National Aeronautics and Space Administration 15. NIMASA: Nigeria Maritime Administration and Safety Agency.
- NIN: National Identity Number
- NIMC: National Identity Management Commission
- POS: Processing Monetary Transactions.
- PSC: Person of Significant Control
- PSS: Payment Solution Services
- PSSP: Payment Solution Services Provider
- PTS: Payment Terminal Services
- PTSP: Payment Terminal Services Provider.

BIBLIOGRAPHY

1. H.Y. Bhadmus: Bhadmus on Corporate Law Practice 4th Edition Nigeria, Chenglo Limited,2017.
2. Nicholas J. P: https://www.diligent.com/insights/corporate-governance
3. The South Sea Bubble. https://www.historicuk.com/history.uk/historyofEngland/south-sea-Bubble
4. Statutes of the United Kingdom, 1825.

www.ingramcontent.com/pod-product-compliance
Lightning Source LLC
Chambersburg PA
CBHW081401130726
47998CB00011B/3035